MW00605117

# TUCKER SIGNING STRATEGIES FOR READING

## Revised Edition

Tucker Signing Strategies for Reading. Revised Edition.
Tucker, Bethanie H., Ed.D.
      164 pp.

© 2001 by Bethanie H. Tucker. Revised 2012.

ISBN-13: 978-1-934583-67-8


1. Reading   2. Education   3. Title


Copyright © 2001 by Bethanie H. Tucker. Revised 2012.
Published by aha! Process, Inc.

All rights reserved. No part of this book may be reproduced in any manner whatsoever
without written permission, except in the case of brief quotations embedded in critical
articles and reviews—and the reproducible student pages in Part II. For information, ad-
dress aha! Process, Inc., P.O. Box 727, Highlands, TX 77562-0727; fax (281) 426-5600.

Copy editing by Jesse Conrad
Book design by Paula Nicolella
Cover design by Frieda Probst


Printed in the United States of America.

# TUCKER SIGNING STRATEGIES FOR READING

## Revised Edition

## Bethanie H. Tucker

Other titles by Bethanie H. Tucker

*Readiness Skills and Relationship Building*
*for Early Childhood Education*

*Vocabulary and Mental Model Development*
*for Early Childhood Education*

*Reading by Age 5*

*Mr. Base Ten Invents Mathematics*

*The Journey of Al and Gebra to the Land of Algebra*

*Understanding and Engaging Under-Resourced College Students*
(K. A. Becker, K. M. Krodel, & B. H. Tucker)

# ACKNOWLEDGMENTS

**Special thanks to:**

Robert Gossom, national educational consultant and Tucker trainer, for contributing the phonics rules for each lesson in the manual.

Kayla Owen, my niece and hand-sign model for this edition of the manual.

Paula Nicolella, desktop publisher, for designing the manual contents.

Frieda Probst graphic designer, for designing the covers.

Peggy Conrad, vice president of publications for aha! Process, for guiding all the rest of us through the process.

Jesse Conrad for his editorial help.

# TABLE OF CONTENTS

# INTRODUCTION

## Phonics Instruction

Learning to read involves recognizing the printed symbols for words and sounds. Children learn to read printed text in a number of ways. Words instantly recognized are part of the child's **sight vocabulary.** The **context** in which a word is found can contribute to one's ability to recognize certain words, such as the word *stop* on a stop sign. Instruction in the acquisition of sight vocabulary and contextual-clue recognition is an essential component of any reading program.

A third vital component of reading instruction is **phonetic analysis.** In order to grasp the fundamentals of the reading process, children must learn that printed letters represent speech sounds. Phonics instruction involves teaching the relationship between printed letters and the speech sounds they represent.

Of the three interrelated reading skills—sight vocabulary, contextual clues, and phonetic analysis—the latter is frequently the most difficult for children to master, primarily because learning letter-sound relationships is totally different from the child's previous life experiences. Additional difficulties stem from the fact that letter shapes are arbitrary and abstract. There is no logical relationship between the appearance of the letter and the sound it represents—no inherent clues to assist the child in remembering the associated sound.

A child attempting to read a word containing the letter *p,* for example, obviously can see the printed letter on the page. His/her task is to remember the speech sound represented by the printed symbol and blend that speech sound with others that surround it. The goal of the signing strategy is to provide a tool to assist the reader in accomplishing this task.

Included in this revised edition of the *Tucker Signing Strategies for Reading* manual are phonics rules applicable to the words in which new signs are introduced. How and under what circumstances the rules are taught is left to the discretion of the teacher. Suggestions for color coding word parts are also included, the use of which is also left to the discretion of the teacher.

## Research Findings

The strategy of signing phonetic sounds has been field-tested with children and adults from a variety of backgrounds in various settings, including one-on-one and large-group instruction in public and private schools—and among home-schooled children and private tutorials. With certain modifications determined by the needs of the child, the program is effective with all populations and in any environment.

Research shows that the signing strategy has been successful in meeting the original goal of the program—to build a bridge between printed symbols and the speech sounds they represent. Children move almost immediately from **learning** the signs to **using** them to decode unfamiliar words. Children who have been taught this strategy frequently are observed moving their hands to decode words when reading for pleasure and when reading from science and social studies texts during silent reading and oral recitations.

In addition to building a bridge between letters and speech sounds, several surprising (yet equally important) benefits have been identified.

1. **Because the signing inherent in the strategy interjects movement into the reading process, many very active students demonstrate the ability and the desire to read for longer blocks of time when using the hand signs.** The reading act naturally includes visual clues in the form of printed words; auditory clues are added when the teacher and the students pro-

nounce the sounds that the printed letters represent. The process is typically devoid, however, of kinesthetic involvement. The Tucker hand signs not only allow for, but actually require, bodily involvement to become part of the reading process. This movement component particularly benefits the child whose preferred learning style is kinesthetic/tactile, which some studies indicate may be as many of 80% of young readers. Whatever the learning style, all children need to move about in order to release excess energy. Although slight, the movement included in hand signing allows for some energy release, enabling the learner to concentrate more intently and for longer periods of time.

2. **Benefits to boys and ADHD students are immediate and dramatic.** Perhaps because most boys are naturally active, and certainly because ADHD (attention deficit hyperactivity disorder) children, the majority of whom are boys, are quite active, these groups of students have demonstrated the most immediate positive reaction to, and appear to have derived the greatest benefits from, the hand signs. Teachers and parents of learning-disabled and mentally challenged children also have reported success with the strategy.

3. **Requiring children to attempt an unfamiliar word using hand signs shifts the onus of responsibility for solving a word from the teacher to the child.** When confronted with an unfamiliar word, beginning readers sometimes stare at an object or look intently at their teachers, waiting for help. By reminding the child to sign the word the teacher is saying, "You have the power to read this word." Children no longer need to wait for someone to do the work for them. This sense of self-empowerment transfers very quickly to new reading situations. The signing strategy identifies tools—the hands—that almost always are readily available to the child.

4. **A surprising result of the Tucker Signing Strategies for Reading has been the degree to which children enjoy using the hand signs.** Many appear to view this experience as learning a special sign language (or even "secret code"), with learning to read an added bonus. They come to enjoy identifying the "special" signs and chunks in words. As a result, they learn to look at the entire word rather than guessing the word based on the initial consonant or syllable. The program also makes learning some phonetic rules less of a burden because the children enjoy making the associated signs.

5. **The signing strategy cues teachers to the students' thought processes.** Children typically reveal very few clues as to what they are thinking as they gaze at an unfamiliar word. The overt behaviors involved in the signing process provide insight for the teacher as to what mental processes are taking place in the child's mind. The requirement to sign is in essence a requirement to think out loud.

6. **Learning the hand signs requires little effort for most children.** The author's initial concern over "adding to the curriculum" proved to be unfounded. Most children of first-grade age or older learn all 44 signs in two or three half-hour sessions. Younger children naturally need to learn the signs and the associated speech sounds at a slower, more developmentally appropriate pace.

7. **Adults report that they benefit from learning the signs.** A number of adults have been taught to read using the Tucker signing strategies. They report that when in an environment where they don't want to use the signs, they can think about them and thereby remember the associated speech sounds.

# TUCKER SIGNING STRATEGIES FOR READING

*Tucker Signing Strategies for Reading* is designed to prompt associations between letters and the sounds they represent. The prompts are hand signs. The program includes a hand sign for each letter and some letter combinations that represent distinct speech sounds. The Tucker hand signs are different from the signs of American Sign Language. Each hand sign is designed to resemble, to the greatest extent possible, the shape and the sound of the letter it represents. The hand sign for the letter *p,* for example, is shaped like the letter *p* and is held in front of the lips as the *p* sound is pronounced. The sign, therefore, builds a bridge between the printed letter and the associated speech sound.

## Guidelines for Teaching Reading Using Hand Signs

1. **All hand signs must be made with the left hand.** Many letter shapes appear backwards when signed with the right hand (see LESSON 1: long *e*). Naturally, some children (and many adults) who are right-handed initially resist using the left hand. Research on the Tucker signing strategies demonstrates that …

    A. Signing with the left hand is not difficult. Right-handed children demonstrate very little if any frustration forming the signs with their left hand. While a few children need to be reminded regularly at first to use their left hand, a quick and casual verbal prompt usually suffices.

    B. After some practice, resistance to left-handed signing quickly diminishes or disappears. Children can be encouraged to use their left hand in a number of ways. Some teachers instruct the children to hold an object in their right hand while signing, which makes it impossible for them to sign with the incorrect hand. Another successful strategy is to provide the children with yarn bracelets that slip easily over their hands—and to which small bells have been tied. The bracelets can be slipped over the right hand, with the warning that no bells should be heard—or over the left hand, with the invitation to "let the signs ring."

    C. After the initial presentation of each sign, the child rarely **looks** at the shape of his/her hand when signing; therefore, the kinesthetic involvement becomes more important than the visual appearance of the letter in sparking the appropriate letter-sound relationship. Thus many teachers choose not to correct children who occasionally forget to use the left hand at this point but are experiencing success decoding words.

2. **Students *must* make the letter speech/ sound(s) as they make each sign.** This simultaneous "signing," "seeing," and "saying" strengthens letter shape/sound associations and creates a multi-modal learning situation.

3. **New signs should be demonstrated in isolation very briefly, then immediately blended with other letters in the context of a word.** When a word is signed, the individual letter signs should be blended into one continuous motion, flowing smoothly from one letter into the next. When signing the word *no,* for example, the *n* sign and *n* sound should be made distinctly, stretching the *n* sound. Then, without breaking the sounds of the word, the left hand should move downward into the *o* sign as the *n* sound blends into the *o* sound, completing the word *no.* Beginning with LESSON 2, each new sound is presented in the context of a word. Each new word and all other words

in the children's story pages in the second half of the manual contain the new letter combined with previously taught letters only, so the child should be able to read each page in the story independently, with the help of the hand signs.

4. **Blends and other common letter combinations should be signed as one unit—or chunk.** These blends—or chunks—should be practiced as a unit whenever they are encountered. When teaching the word *horse,* for example, the teacher would point out the *or* chunk, and students would practice signing *or* several times. The teacher also would prompt students to recognize the silent *e* at the end of the word. The word would then be signed *h-or-s* (silent *e*). Students should later be prompted to recognize the *or* chunk in additional words. Other word chunks to point out and practice include *oy, oi,* and consonant blends. When teaching the word *brisk,* for example, the *br* blend should be recognized and practiced, then the *sk* blend addressed. The reason the letter *i* represents the short-*i* sound should subsequently be discussed. Finally, the word *brisk* would be signed *br-i-sk.* Tucker hand signs have been formulated for certain very distinctive word chunks, such as *tion, sh, ch, ow, ou,* and *r*-controlled vowels.

5. **Students should *discontinue* use of the hand signs when they are reading immediately recognizable words.** The researcher was initially concerned about students relying too heavily on the hand signs, allowing them to become permanent crutches. This concern also was unfounded. Children automatically drop the hand signs upon recognition of a word or words. On many occasions a child will need to sign only one word in a sentence—or perhaps only a portion of a word. If, for example, a student can read the *see* portion of the word *seeing,* he/she should be encouraged to read *see,* sign *ing,* then put the word parts together and solve the word.

6. **Rules of phonetic analysis must be taught.** The Tucker hand signs assist children in recalling letter-sound relationships and blending sounds to make words. They do not, however, hold any secrets for teaching phonetic rules, other than the fact that the hand signs sometimes make learning rules more fun. Research demonstrates, for example, that many children enjoy decoding words that end with silent *e* using the signing strategy because they enjoy making the silent-*e* sign. Many children also enjoy looking for special signable chunks in a word before they attempt to read it. This level of enjoyment can occur only after rules have been taught through both the signing strategy **and** those strategies that teachers typically employ.

7. **Long-vowel sounds are presented before short vowels.** Because long-vowel sounds "say" the vowel names and therefore are easier for children to remember, they are presented before short vowels in this manual. Signs for long-vowel sounds are basically the same as short-vowel signs. Long-vowel signs *a, e,* and *o* are made at waist level; the short-vowel signs are made with the hand held higher in the air.

   Similar modifications apply to *i, y,* and *u.* More detailed explanations are provided in the lessons in which these letters are presented.

8. **Irregularly spelled words can be handled a number of ways.**

   A. Words that are frequently encountered and do not follow regular spelling rules should be presented as sight vocabulary, with a brief explanation that they break the rules of phonetics and, therefore, cannot be signed.

Examples of **SIGHT VOCABULARY WORDS** include:

| | | | | |
|------|--------|---------|------|------|
| does | done | friends | give | have |
| here | know | love | many | more |
| none | of | once | one | put |
| said | should | snow | some | to |
| two | use | who | you | your |

B. When only a portion of the word contains an irregular spelling pattern, this "tricky part" can be pointed out and pronounced for the child, and the remainder of the word can be signed. An example would be the word *naughty.* It could be pointed out that the *gh* in this word is silent. Then the remainder of the word can be signed *n-au-t* and *y* (*e* sound).

C. Families of words that contain irregular spelling patterns, such as *igh,* can be taught in one lesson. When presenting the word *light,* for example, the teacher would explain that the *gh* combination is silent, and the *i* sign will be made when *igh* is encountered. The word would then be signed with the *L,* long-*i,* and *t* signs. Additional words that belong to this word family should then be presented.

D. Minimal-contrast sounds, such as the *zh* sound in *pleasure* and the distinction between the voiced and unvoiced *th* sound, should be acknowledged with little elaboration at this point. When teaching the word *pleasure,* for example, the teacher could simply say, "That *s* sounds a little like a *z,* doesn't it?" Children tend to accept these irregularities readily.

# MANUAL FORMAT

Part I of this manual is divided into 44 lessons, with one new hand sign introduced in each lesson. The lessons are sequenced for the emergent reader but can be rearranged or accelerated for more advanced readers.

Each lesson includes:

1. **A description and illustration of the new hand sign.**

2. **Procedures for teaching the lesson.**

3. **Extension and enrichment activities.** These activities suggest strategies for reinforcing each new letter sign. Although most activities are listed only once, many can be repeated for a number of letter signs. For example, the PICTURE DICTIONARY described in LESSON 2 could be continued for each new letter. Such activities as WATER WRITING described in LESSON 3 and SLOW RACE in LESSON 9 also can be repeated frequently. WORD CHALLENGE words, which are listed for most lessons, combine each new sign with previously taught letters to form new words, in addition to those found in the story.

4. **Student Take-Home Book Title.** Each lesson references a Student Take-Home Book with controlled vocabulary. These books are available through aha! Process, Inc. in a reproducible workbook format for students to read and take home.

Part II includes story pages that feature each lesson's focus word(s) in the context of previously taught words and letters. Each student page, which is to be illustrated by the student, contributes to an ongoing story. Student pages should be hole-punched and added to each child's individual storybook as they are completed.

# BEGINNING THE PROGRAM

## Emergent Readers

When working with children ages 5 and younger who are ready to learn to read, many teachers cover the first five or six lessons quickly, perhaps in one session. On Day 2 the previously taught letters can be reviewed and one or two new ones added. This approach sustains interest and allows students to feel an immediate sense of accomplishment, having learned to read several words in a short period of time.

## More Advanced/Older Readers

More mature readers may not need to complete each lesson in its entirety and certainly will not need to complete every **extension** and **enrichment** activity suggested in the manual. More advanced readers would be expected to move quickly through individual letter signs, progressing immediately to blends, diphthongs, digraphs, affixes, and

other word chunks. It is often more appealing to older readers to begin with the blends as opposed to the simpler signs, so that they can immediately read longer and more challenging words.

More advanced readers enjoy quickly learning the signs and using them to attack longer, more sophisticated words that follow regular spelling patterns. These words can be approached in a fashion similar to the way a detective would look for clues to solve a case. When attempting to solve these words, the reader should first identify such clues as blends, affixes, digraphs, diphthongs, *r*-controlled vowels, and other word chunks. The word *church,* for example, contains three word chunks: *ch, ur,* and *ch,* which the child could identify, sign, blend, and pronounce.

The list of regularly spelled words that appeal to children beyond the kindergarten level is virtually endless. Following is an introductory list:

| | | | | |
|---|---|---|---|---|
| aardvark | abash | abbreviation | abdomen | abduct |
| abduction | abide | ablaze | abound | abrupt |
| absorb | absorption | absurd | acceleration | accommodation |
| account | accumulation | action | activate | adder |
| addiction | addition | administration | admiration | admirer |
| admonition | adoption | adoration | adore | adorn |
| adverb | adverse | advertise | affection | affliction |
| afterburner | aftermath | afterward | aggravation | aground |
| ajar | alarm | alert | alive | allegation |
| allergic | alligator | allow | aloud | alternation |
| alternator | arch | auburn | auction | audit |
| auditory | augur | august | author | automatic |
| aviation | awkward | awning | battery | baud |
| bawl | bluster | bookkeeper | bracket | bravery |
| broker | caption | carbon | carp | carpenter |
| catcher | category | caucus | cauliflower | causation |
| cause | caustic | caution | chamber | chapter |
| char | chart | charter | cheddar | chew |
| chide | chirp | church | churn | coach |

continued on next page

continued from previous page

| | | | | |
|---|---|---|---|---|
| condition | confer | confine | confirm | convene |
| cower | crawl | cub | cube | cucumber |
| cutlery | cyclone | dawn | dermis | dervish |
| description | dinner | discord | dock | docket |
| edit | elevator | emotion | endive | erode |
| erupt | eruption | ether | ethic | expectation |
| expert | faucet | Faulkner | fault | fauna |
| fawn | femur | fender | fever | finite |
| flirt | flitter | flower | foundation | fraction |
| further | garland | gauze | gawk | govern |
| grant | grip | gripe | grist | hack |
| haul | haunt | hawk | hawker | Hawthorne |
| hermit | hinder | housekeeping | hyper | impart |
| incurs | induction | intercept | jaunt | jawbone |
| jury | landmark | landslide | larder | larva |
| laud | launch | launcher | laundry | laurel |
| lawful | lawless | lawyer | lease | liberty |
| lifelike | lobster | location | locomotion | lodestone |
| lotion | loud | makeshift | maul | medicate |
| mineral | motivation | muffler | nation | nausea |
| nautical | observation | option | orderly | otter |
| ouch | ounce | outbound | outburst | outcurve |
| outer | outgoing | outlaw | outline | outrun |
| outskirts | outstanding | outstation | outward | overcast |
| overhand | owl | parch | partner | partnership |
| Pauline | pauper | pause | pawn | penetrate |
| penicillin | peninsula | percolate | phase | poncho |
| pouch | pounce | poverty | power | prevent |
| proceed | profile | propose | prosper | Quaker |
| quarter | quartile | question | quiver | quota |
| quote | raw | recede | refer | release |
| resolute | return | rout | rubbish | rudder |
| sanction | saucer | sauna | sausage | saw |
| sawhorse | sawyer | scalp | scorch | score |
| scowl | scratch | sector | sharpen | shatter |
| sheepskin | shelve | shimmer | shirt | shower |
| shun | sling | sober | soccer | squawk |
| squelch | squint | squirm | squirt | stampede |
| starvation | substance | substitute | sunshine | taunt |
| tawny | temper | thermos | thorn | tilt |
| timber | tower | trickery | turnover | urchin |
| vacation | valve | vanish | vapor | vault |
| vaulted | violent | viper | vitamin | vivid |
| vocation | voice | volunteer | voucher | warn |
| warning | warp | wart | waste | wave |

continued on next page

continued from previous page

| | | | | |
|---|---|---|---|---|
| whiff | whimper | whirl | whiskers | whisper |
| wince | wintergreen | Yale | yam | yammer |
| yard | yarn | yawl | yawn | yestermorning |
| yippee | yodel | yoke | yolk | yucca |
| Yukon | zenith | zero | zigzag | zing |
| ZIP code | zipper | zippy | zone | zoom |

When irregularly spelled words are presented to readers of all ages, the "tricky parts" (letters or letter combinations that do not follow regular pronunciation rules) should be pointed out before the child attempts the word.

## Phonetic Organizer

Some children benefit from a phonetic organizer, such as a chart that lists the most frequent spellings of each vowel sound. The example below shows how a chart might look in its initial states; additional spellings and examples should be added to the chart as they are encountered.

| a | | | e | | | | | i | | |
|---|---|---|---|---|---|---|---|---|---|---|
| a (e) | cake | | e | me | ey | key | | i (e) | kite | |
| ay | day | | ee | see | ie | chief | | y | my | |
| ey | they | | ea | meat | y | pony | | igh | sight | |

| o | | | u | | | | |
|---|---|---|---|---|---|---|---|
| o | no | | u (e) | cute | | | |
| o (e) | bone | | ue | glue | | | |
| ow | show | | ew | flew | | | |
| oa | boat | | | | | | |

In each case, the represented sound is signed. For example, when signing the word *say*, the *ay* would be signed with the long-*a* sign. The word *light* would be signed *L, long-i, t.*

# Part I

# TUCKER SIGNING STRATEGIES FOR READING

## Lessons 1-44

# LESSON 1 – long *e*

*Note: All letters should be signed with the left hand. If signed with the right hand, many letters, including the letter* e, *would face in the wrong direction.*

## Sign Description

Curl the fingers of your left hand to resemble the shape of the letter *e,* as illustrated. Then extend your hand outward while making the long-*e* sound.

 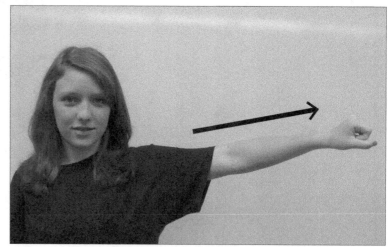

(always use left hand)

## Procedures

1. When demonstrating the long-*e* sign, the teacher should draw the letter *e* on his/her left hand with a washable marker.

2. Instruct students to look at the sign and make the *e* sound as they sign the letter. (Making the sound is a vital part of each sign and should be repeated for every letter.)

## Student Page – #1

**TEXT:** eeeee

**ILLUSTRATION:** Draw a picture of yourself and something that frightens you and makes you say "eeeee."

## Extension Activity

GIVE ME A SIGN: As the teacher reads a list of words, the students make the *e* sign (and sound) when they hear a word that contains the long-*e* sound. Sample words containing the long-*e* sound include *bead, bean, bee, breeze, believe, clean, dream, feed, he, me, mean, neat, need, season, see, seed, seen, she,* and *we.*

## Enrichment Activity

HAND PAINTING: Instruct students to **paint** the letter *e* on their left hand using safe products, such as finger paint, chalk, pudding, etc.

## Student Take-Home Book—*eeeee*

# LESSON 2 – *m*

## Sign Description

Extend the three middle fingers of your left hand downward to resemble the letter *m*, as illustrated in Step 1. Place the tips of your extended fingers to your lips while making the *m* sound.

## Procedures

1. Trace the *m* shape on your hand with a washable marker.

2. Demonstrate the *m* sign; instruct students to make the *m* sound as they sign the letter.

3. Review the *e* sign.

4. Demonstrate signing the letter *m*, stretching the *m* sound and flowing smoothly into the *e* sign and sound to form the word *me*. There should not be a break between the *m* sound and the *e* sound.

## Applicable Phonics Rule

**Phonics Rule 1:** When a word (or syllable) has only one vowel which comes at the end of the word (or syllable), the vowel is usually long. E.g., *me, tiger.* Color code *e* in *me* and *i* in *tiger* red.

## Student Page – #2

**TEXT:** Me

**ILLUSTRATION:** Draw a picture of yourself.

## Extension Activities

**FOOD CHAIN:** Read a list of foods. Students respond to their favorites by making the *m* sign and *m* sound.

**PICTURE DICTIONARY:** Students will find magazine pictures of objects that begin with the letter *m* and glue the pictures to a page labeled *m*. Repeat this activity for subsequent lessons and combine pages to make PICTURE DICTIONARIES.

## Enrichment Activity

**SLOW SIGNS:** Instruct the students to slowly sign the word *me* as one child writes it on the board. Repeat as additional children do the writing.

## Student Take-Home Book—*Me?*

# LESSON 3 – *s*

**Previously taught letters:** long *e*, *m*

**Lesson focus word:** *See*

## Sign Description

Draw the *s* shape in the air while making the *s* sound. Making the *s* shape with all fingers extended allows for smoother blending and word formation than drawing with the index finger only.

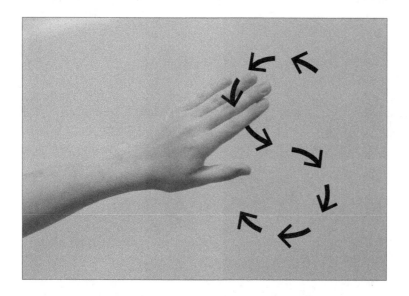

## Procedures

1. Demonstrate the *s* sign.

2. Instruct students to make the *s* sound as they sign the letter.

3. Review the *e* sign and the word *me*.

4. Demonstrate blending the letter signs for *s* and *e* to form the word *see*. (The *e* sign should be made only once when signing the word *see*, even though the letter *e* appears twice.)

## Applicable Phonics Rule

**Phonics Rule 2:** When two vowels come together, the first one says its name, and the second one gets quiet. E.g., *beat, seem.* Color code the two vowels together red, which means ***stop*** and ***think.***

## Student Page – #3

**TEXT:** See me.

**ILLUSTRATION:** Draw a picture of yourself doing something exciting.

## Extension Activities

**PICTURE DICTIONARY:** See LESSON 2.

**WATER WRITING:** Instruct students to slowly make the *s* sign as one child writes the letter *s* on the board using a paintbrush and water. Repeat with additional children water writing.

**WORD CHALLENGE:** Discuss the meaning of the word *seem* and demonstrate how it would be signed.

## Enrichment Activities

**STRING ART:** Instruct students to draw a large letter *S* on a sheet of paper, then glue string over the shape.

***SEE ME*** **BOOKLET:** Ask students to find magazine pictures of someone doing something exciting. Cover the face of the person in the magazine picture with a snapshot or self-portrait of the child's face. Students then glue the picture to the bottom half of a sheet of paper and write *See Me* across the top.

## Student Take-Home Book—*See Me*

# LESSON 4 – *w*

**Previously taught letters:** long *e, m, s*

**Lesson focus word:** *We*

## Sign Description

Extend the three middle fingers of your left hand upward to resemble the letter *w*. Draw the letter *w* on your fingers with a washable marker. Then place the tips of the extended fingers to your throat as you make the *w* sound.

## Procedures

1. Demonstrate the *w* sign; instruct students to make the *w* sound as the sign is made.

2. Review the *e* sign.

3. Demonstrate blending the *w* sign with the *e* sign to form the word *we*.

## Student Page – #4

**TEXT:** We see.

**ILLUSTRATION:** Draw a picture of yourself doing something exciting while two of your friends are watching.

## Extension Activities

**PICTURE DICTIONARY:** Continue with each lesson (see LESSON 2).

***WE* OR *ME*?** Make flash cards with the words *we* and *me* written in various sizes and colors. The students will sign the appropriate word when it is flashed.

**WORD CHALLENGE** (in this and subsequent lessons, allow students to tackle WORD CHALLENGE words independently before offering assistance; discuss word meanings as necessary): *wee.*

## Enrichment Activities

**3-D HANDS:** Trace and cut out a silhouette of your left hand. Draw the letter w on the three middle fingers of your cutout. Roll the thumb and pinky to the back of your cutout, then glue the tips of these two fingers together, creating a 3-D representation of the *w* sign. Display on a board labeled "See What **We** Have Done."

**SEASONAL SIGNS:** Point out that the word *summer* begins with the letter *s* and the word *winter* begins with the letter *w.* Read a list of activities that might be performed during one of the two seasons. Students respond with the *w* sign for wintertime activities and with the *s* sign for summertime activities. Suggested activities might include making a snowman, swimming, building a fire in the fireplace, going barefoot, wearing a woolly coat, etc.

***WE SEE* BOOKLET:** Make booklets similar to the *See Me* booklet described for LESSON 3, substituting the words "We See _____" and filling in the blank with the child's name.

## Student Take-Home Book—*We See*

# LESSON 5 – short *u*

**Previously taught letters:** long *e, m, s, w*

**Lesson focus word:** *Us*

## Sign Description

Form the *u* shape with your left hand, as illustrated. Draw
the shape of the letter on your hand with a washable marker.
Touch your thumb to the underside of your chin while making
the short-*u* sound.

## Procedures

1. Demonstrate the short-*u* sign, making the short-*u* sound as the sign is made.

2. Review the *s* sign.

3. Demonstrate blending the short-*u* and *s* signs to make the word *us*.

## Applicable Phonics Rule

**Phonics Rule 3**: When a word (or syllable) has only one vowel coming between consonants, the vowel is usually short. E.g., *nut, sample.*

## Student Page – #5

**TEXT**: See us.

**ILLUSTRATION**: Draw a picture of yourself having fun with two friends.

## Extension Activities

**WORD CHALLENGE** (discuss plural forms of words): *mum, mums, muss, sum, sums* (approximate the *s* sound in the words *sums* and *mums*).

**IT'S YOUR GUESS**: Have students, one at a time, sign a WORD CHALLENGE word. Let other students guess the word that is being signed.

## Enrichment Activities

*SEE US* **BOOKLET**: Follow the procedure for the *See Me* booklet (LESSON 3).

**UMBRELLA** *U's*: Students will draw a large upper-case *U*, then invert the letter and embellish it to resemble an umbrella. Discuss the *u* sound at the beginning of the word *umbrella.*

## Student Take-Home Book—*See Us*

# LESSON 6 – long *i*

**Previously taught letters:** long *e, m, s, w,* short *u,*

**Lesson focus word:** *I* (as a word)

## Sign Description

Draw the letter *i* on your index finger with a washable marker. Point to your left eye, with your index finger pointing straight upward, and then extend your hand forward while making the long-*i* sound.

## Procedures

1. Demonstrate the long-*i* sign, making the long-*i* sound as the sign is made.

2. Review the *s* and long-*e* signs and the word *see.*

## Student Page – #6

**TEXT:** I see …

**ILLUSTRATION:** Draw a picture of yourself looking at something behind a rock. Your friends are waiting for you to tell them what you see.

## Extension Activities

**I SEE YOU:** One student at a time stands in front of the room with the words *I see* written over his/her head on the board. The class in unison signs *I see* _____, filling in the blank with the child's name.

## Enrichment Activity

*"I See …"* (played similarly to "I Spy"). One child will sign the words *I see,* then end the sentence with a description of something he/she sees as the others guess the identity of the object.

## Student Take-Home Book—*I See*

# LESSON 7 – *b*

## Sign Description

Make a straight line with your left hand, as illustrated. Move the left hand back and forth, imitating a bat striking an imaginary ball, while making the *b* sound. (Emphasize that the straight line in the letter *b* comes before the circle. This helps the children to differentiate more easily between the *b* and the *d*.)

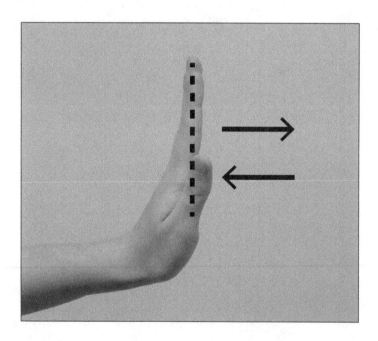

## Procedures

1. Demonstrate the *b* sign; make the *b* sound as the sign is made.

2. Review the *e* and *s* signs; blend to make the word *bees*. Comment that the letter *s* sounds slightly different in the word *bees* from how it sounds in the word *see*.

3. Discuss the word *bees*.

TEXT: bees!

ILLUSTRATION: Draw a picture of bees flying over your head.

## Extension Activities

BOARD WRITING (extension activities for the letter *b* should emphasize the fact that the straight line is written before the circle): Have two students go to the board. The first student draws the straight line, while the second student makes the *b* sign. The teacher or another child adds the circle to complete the letter *b*.

WORD CHALLENGE: *bum, bums, bus, sub, subs*

## Enrichment Activity

HANDPRINTS: Brush finger paints onto the outside of the child's hand. The child presses the painted side of his/her hand to a sheet of paper, making the straight-line portion of the letter *b*. The circle can be added with a paintbrush, marker, printing tool, etc.

## Student Take-Home Book—*Bees See*

# LESSON 8 – *n* (and silent *e*)

**Previously taught letters:** long *e, m, s, w,* short *u,* long *i, b*

**Lesson focus word:** *Nine*

## Sign Description

Extend the index and middle fingers of your left hand downward, as illustrated in Step 1. Draw the letter *n* on the fingers with a washable marker. Place the tips of the extended fingers on your chin (Step 2). Pull downward on the chin slightly to emphasize the parting of your lips as you make the *n* sound.

## Procedures

1. Demonstrate the *n* sign, making the *n* sound as the sign is made.

2. Review the word *bees* and the long-*i* sound.

3. Demonstrate blending the *n,* long-*i, n,* and silent-*e* sounds to make the word *nine.*

## Applicable Phonics Rule

**Phonics Rule 4:** When a single vowel is followed by one consonant and a final *e*, the first vowel is usually long, and the final *e* is silent. E.g., *mate, take*. Color code the silent-*e* words orange, and tell children the *e* has magic powers that make the first vowel say its name while the *e* stays silent. When a silent *e* is encountered, students can place their right hands over their left fists to symbolize that the *e* is silent.

## Student Page – #8

**TEXT:** Nine bees …

**ILLUSTRATION:** Draw a picture of nine bees.

## Extension Activities

**WORD CHALLENGE:** *bun, buns, mine, nub, nubs, nun, nuns, seen, sun, suns, swine, wine*

**CHALK SPELLING:** Slowly sign and pronounce words previously covered as the students write the words on individual chalkboards. When finished writing, each child holds up his/her board to be checked.

## Enrichment Activity

**NINE PICTURES:** Instruct students to clip nine pictures of a particular object, such as nine cars, trees, etc. Then direct students to glue the pictures to a page labeled "Nine _____." Write the word that names their pictures in the blank for them, pointing out any previously covered letters.

## Student Take-Home Book—*Nine Swine*

# LESSON 9 – *z*

**Previously taught letters:** long *e, m, s, w,* short *u,* long *i, b, n* (and silent *e*)

**Lesson focus word:** *Buzz*

## Sign Description

Draw the *z* shape in the air with your left hand, as illustrated.

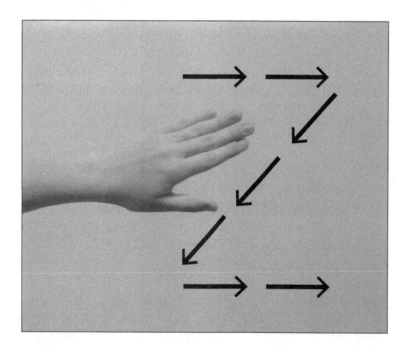

## Procedures

1. Demonstrate the *z* sign, making the *z* sound as the sign is made.

2. Review the *b* and short-*u* signs.

3. Demonstrate blending the *b, u,* and *z* signs to make the word *buzz.*

## Applicable Phonics Rule

**Phonics Rule 5:** When two identical (or twin) consonants follow a short vowel sound, we give only one consonant sound. E.g., *buzz*.

## Student Page – #9

**TEXT:** buzz.

**ILLUSTRATION:** Draw a picture of some bees, then write the word *buzz* beside each one.

## Extension Activity

**SLOW RACE:** Conduct a **race** to see who can draw the letter *z* in the air the slowest, while making the *z* sound. Call time after one minute. Anyone who is still drawing the letter *z* and making the z sound when time is called is a winner.

## Enrichment Activities

**BUZZ:** Read a list of words. When the students hear a word that begins with the letter *z*, they should make the *z* sign and sound. *Z* words might include *zeal, zebra, zenith, zero, zest, zigzag, zip, ZIP code, zipper, zodiac, zone, zoo,* and *zoom.*

**ZZZZZ:** Instruct students to find magazine pictures of people sleeping. Have them clip and glue the pictures to a sheet of paper. Explain that when some people snore they sometimes make a *z* sound. Instruct your students to draw several letter *z*'s over the picture of the sleeping person.

## Student Take-Home Book—*Buzz, Buzz, Buzz*

# LESSON 10 – *r*

**Previously taught letters:** long *e, m, s, w,* short *u,* long *i, b, n* (and silent *e*), *z*

**Lesson focus word:** *Run*

## Sign Description

Draw a large lower-case *r* on the board. Trace the curved portion of the *r* with your left hand, as illustrated, while making the *r* sound.

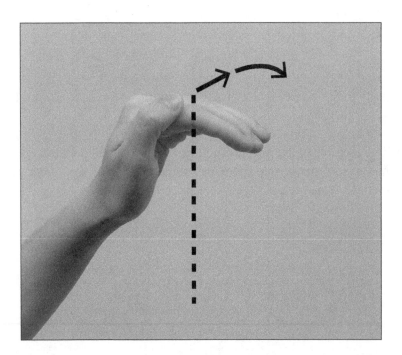

## Procedures

1. Demonstrate the *r* sign, making the *r* sound as the sign is made.

2. Review the *u* and *n* signs.

3. Demonstrate blending the *r, u,* and *n* signs and sounds to make the word *run*.

## Student Page – #10

*Note: Introduce the upper-case* R *before presenting the student page.*

**TEXT:** Run, run!

**ILLUSTRATION:** Draw a picture of you and your friends running away from the bees.

## Extension Activities

**CHEERS:** Discuss cheering at a ballgame. In cheerleader style call out, "Give me an (make the *r* sign and sound)." The children will respond with the *r* sign and sound. Repeat for a *u* and an *n*. Then ask, "What did I spell?" Repeat the procedure for previously covered words.

**WORD CHALLENGE:** *rub, rubs*

## Enrichment Activity

**RAINBOW *R's*:** Point out that the top part of the letter *r* (the part that is drawn when signing the letter) is shaped like a rainbow. Instruct the children to clip *r* words from magazines or newspapers and glue them to the rainbow-shaped portion of a large letter *r*.

## Student Take-Home Book—*Nine Rats*

# LESSON 11 – *p*

## Sign Description

Form a *p* shape with your left hand, as illustrated. Draw the letter *p* on your hand with a washable marker. Place the circular portion of the letter *p* in front of your lips as you make the *p* sound.

## Procedures

1. Demonstrate the *p* sign while making the *p* sound.

2. Review the *u* sign.

3. Demonstrate blending the short-*u* and *p* signs to make the word *up*.

## Phonics Reminder

When signing words from the WORD CHALLENGE list, review phonics rules 2, 3, and 4 and continue to use color coding.

## Student Page – #11

TEXT: Run up!

ILLUSTRATION: Draw a picture of you and your friends running up a hill.

## Extension Activities

WORD CHALLENGE: *bump, peep, peeps, pine, pipe, pipes, prime, prize, pump, pup, pups, ripe, weep, weeps, wipe*

LINE UP: Write each letter of the word *pipe* on an individual index card. Call four students to the front of the room and give each student one card. Line up the students so their cards will spell *pipe*. Without telling the word, have the first student make the *p* sign (sound included), the next make the long-*i* sign, the next make the *p* sign, and the last put his/her right hand over the left hand to represent the silent *e*. Let the class guess the word. Repeat the procedure for additional WORD CHALLENGE words.

PIPE-CLEANER *P's*: Instruct students to make large *p* shapes using pipe cleaners. As you read a list of words, students use the pipe-cleaner *p*'s rather than their hands to make the *p* sign and sound when they hear a word that begins with the letter *p*.

## Enrichment Activities

PLEASE PASS THE *P's*: Students will glue dried peas to an outline of the letter *p*. Label the display "Please Pass the *P*'s."

GUESS THE *P* WORD: One student leaves the room while the rest of the class selects an object in the room that begins with the letter *p*. The excused student returns and walks around the room. The remaining students make the *p* sign (and sound) softly when the student is far away from the selected object—and loudly when he/she is close to it—until the object is identified.

## Student Take-Home Book—*Pup*

# LESSON 12 – long *o*

**Previously taught letters:** long *e, m, s, w, short u,* long *i, b, n* (and silent *e*), *z, r, p*

**Lesson focus word:** *No*

## Sign Description

Form an *o* shape with the left hand, as illustrated. Then extend your hand outward while making the long-*o* sound.

## Procedures

1. Demonstrate the long-*o* sign, making the long-*o* sound as the sign is made.

2. Review the *n* sign.

3. Demonstrate blending the *n* and *o* signs to make the word *no.*

4. Demonstrate blending the long-*o* and *r* signs to sign the *or* sound.

## Applicable Phonics Rule

**Phonics Rule 6:** When *s* comes between two vowels, it usually gives the sound of *z*. E.g., *nose, rose*. Color code the *s* in red, and ask children what red means. Explain to them that they have to remember that when *s* comes between two vowels, it usually gives the sound of *z*.

## Student Page – #12

*Note: Discuss the upper-case* I *before presenting the student page.*

**TEXT:** I see no bees.

**ILLUSTRATION:** Draw a picture of you and your friends at the top of the hill. You are happy because there are no bees there.

## Extension Activities

**WORD CHALLENGE:** *bone, more, nose, or, pope, pose, robe, rope, rose, so, sore, wore, zone*

**MORE *OR*s:** Explain that the *or* sound is found in many words and should be recognized and signed fluently as a word chunk. Direct the students to sign the *or* portion of the following words quickly and fluently, as a word chunk rather than as two separate letters: *bore, more, nor, or, pore, sore, wore.*

**YES/NO GAME:** Ask a series of yes/no questions. Students will **sign** *no* or **say** *yes* in response to the questions.

## Enrichment Activities

**CHEERIO:** List the WORD CHALLENGE words on the board. Give each child a small handful of Cheerios. Instruct them to write WORD CHALLENGE words, using cereal for the letter *o*.

**E-I-E-I-O:** Sing "Old McDonald," signing the *e, i, e, i, o* portion of the song.

## Student Take-Home Book—*Sore Pup*

# LESSON 13 – long *a*

**Previously taught letters:** long *e, m, s, w,* short *u,* long *i, b, n* (and silent *e*), *z, r, p,* long *o*

**Lesson focus word:** *A* (as a word)

## Sign Description

Rotate your hand in a counterclockwise direction as if repeatedly tracing the circular part of the letter *a* with the palm of your hand while making the long-*a* sound. (A counterclockwise direction should be followed because this is the direction used for writing the letter *a.*) The sign for the long-*a* sound should be made with the left arm extended outward, away from your body.

## Procedures

1. Demonstrate the long-*a* sign, making the long-*a* sound as the sign is made.

2. Review the words *I* and *see.* Sign and read the word *pup* with the class. Discuss the meaning of the word *pup* as an abbreviated form of *puppy.*

## Applicable Phonics Rule

**Phonics Rule 7:** When *y* comes at the end of a word, it is a vowel. Therefore, *ay* at the end of a word has the long-*a* sound and follows Phonics Rule 2: When two vowels come together, the first one says its name, and the second one gets *quiet*.

## Student Page – #13

**TEXT:** I see a pup.

**ILLUSTRATION:** Draw a picture of a puppy.

## Extension Activities

**CHART ART:** Explain that the long-*a* sign is shown the same way for all spellings. Make a chart listing other common ways to spell the long-*a* sound. (This activity should be repeated for other vowel sounds at the appropriate time.)

| Long *a* | |
|---|---|
| *ai* | *ay* |
| brain | bay |
| main | may |
| pain | pray |
| rain | ray |
| Spain | say |

**WORD CHALLENGE:** *ape, bare, base, bay, brain, main, mane, mare, may, name, pain, pane, pare, pray, rain, ray, same, sane, say, Zane*

## Enrichment Activity

**WHAT DO YOU SEE?** Write the words "I see a _____" on the board. Ask questions, such as "What do you see that is blue?" One student will sign *I see a* _____, then fill in the blank with something he/she sees that is blue.

## Student Take-Home Book—*Zane*

# LESSON 14 – *h*

**Previously taught letters:** long *e, m, s, w,* short *u,* long *i, b, n* (and silent *e*), *z, r, p,* long *o,* long *a*

**Lesson focus word:** *Hi*

## Sign Description

Shape your left hand to resemble the letter *h,* as illustrated. Draw an *h* on your hand with a washable marker. Then position your hand in front of your mouth as you make the *h* sound.

## Procedures

1. Demonstrate the *h* sign, making the *h* sound as the sign is made.

2. Review the long-*i* sign.

3. Demonstrate blending the *h* and *i* signs to make the word *hi.*

## Phonics Reminder

Review phonics rules and color coding as appropriate and needed when decoding words from the WORD CHALLENGE list.

## Student Page – #14

*Note: Introduce upper-case* H *before beginning the student page.*

**TEXT**: Hi, pup.

**ILLUSTRATION**: Draw a picture of yourself petting the pup.

## Extension Activities

**WORD CHALLENGE:** *hay, he, hoe, ho-hum, home, homes, hope, hose, hub, hump, humps*

**FILL-IN-THE-BLANKS LISTENING ACTIVITY** (read the following list of words, omitting the beginning *h* sound; students will add the *h* sign and sound and pronounce the word): *hair, hall, halo, ham, hammer, hamster, hand, hang, happy, hard, harm, harp, hat, he, head, hear, heart, heat, hello, help, her, hiccup, high, hill, hog, hold, home, honey, hop, hope, horn, horse, hose, hot, house, hungry, hunt, hum,* and *hurry.*

## Enrichment Activity

**HI HO, HI HO:** Sing the *Snow White* song … *Hi ho, hi ho; it's off to work we go.* Students will make the *h* sign whenever they hear the *h* sound. Following the song, students may sign the words *hi* and *ho.*

## Student Take-Home Book—*Pup Sees*

# LESSON 15 – *y* (long *i*)

**Previously taught letters:** long *e*, *m*, *s*, *w*, short *u*, long *i*, *b*, *n* (and silent *e*), *z*, *r*, *p*, long *o*, long *a*, *h*

**Lesson focus word:** *My*

## Sign Description

Draw an imaginary *y* shape on your thumb, index finger, and palm. Point to your eye with your index finger, then extend your hand forward while making the long-*i* sound.

## Procedures

1. Demonstrate the *y* sign; make the long-*i* sound as the sign is made.

2. Review the *m* sign.

3. Demonstrate blending the *m* and *y* as long-*i* signs to make the word *my*.

40

## Applicable Phonics Rule

**Phonics Rule 8:** When *y* comes at the end of a word and it is the only vowel, *y* says long *i*. E.g., *by, shy, try.*

## Student Page – #15

**TEXT:** I see my horse.

**ILLUSTRATION:** Draw a picture of you and your horse.

## Extension Activities

**MY, MY, MY:** Students show something that belongs to them as they sign *my* and then name the object they are showing.

**WORD CHALLENGE:** *by, pry, spy*

**BY WHOM?** Instruct students to write the word *by* in front of their name on their paper.

## Enrichment Activities

**MY _____:** Students will draw a picture of something that belongs to them and label the picture "My _____" (naming the object in the blank).

**OR WHAT?** Point out the *or* sound in the word *horse.* Practice signing the word *or* until it becomes automatic. Remind students that *or* should be signed as a unit when encountered in words.

## Student Take-Home Book—*Mine, Mine, Mine!*

# LESSON 16 – *d*

**Previously taught letters:** long *e, m, s, w,* short *u,* long *i, b, n* (and silent *e*), *z, r, p,* long *o,* long *a, h, y* (long-*i* sound)

**Lesson focus word:** *Ride*

## Sign Description

Form an *o* shape with your left hand. Make a circular "digging" motion with your left hand, as illustrated. (Emphasize that the circle in the letter *d* comes before the straight line. This helps the children to differentiate more easily between the *b* and the *d*.)

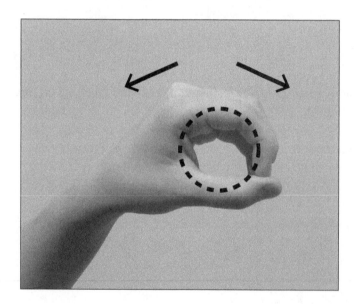

## Procedures

1. Demonstrate the *d* sign and make the *d* sound as the sign is made.

2. Review the *r* and long-*i* signs, as well as the silent-*e* concept.

3. Demonstrate blending the *r,* long-*i,* and *d* signs to make the word *ride.*

## Student Page – #16

**TEXT:** Ride my horse.

**ILLUSTRATION:** Draw a picture of you and your friends riding your horse.

## Extension Activities

*Note: In order to help students differentiate between the* b *and the* d, *it's important for extension activities to emphasize the fact that the circular, digging portion of the letter* d *is written first.*

**DIGGING UP *D's*:** Bury items that begin with the letter *d* in a sand bucket. Allow students to dig for and identify each item, making the *d* sign as each item is named.

**WORD CHALLENGE:** *bud, dame, day, deem, deep, dime, dine, doe, drape* (chunk the *dr* in *drape*) *drum, dump, hide, made, mud, rode, seed, side, suds, wade, weed, wide*

## Enrichment Activity

**DONUTS AND CARROTS** (instruct the students to wash their hands before beginning this activity): Give each child a paper towel, a donut, and a carrot. Students will arrange the donut and the carrot on the paper towel to form a *d* shape. Emphasize the fact that the donut (which they probably like better) comes before the carrot and that the donut begins with the *d* sound. Allow students to eat their letter *d* after they have made the *d* sign.

## Student Take-Home Book—*My Horse Runs*

# LESSON 17 – *g*

*Note: The hard* g *is presented in this lesson. The soft-*g *sound is discussed in the Appendix.*

**Previously taught letters:** long *e, m, s, w,* short *u,* long *i, b, n* (and silent *e*), *z, r, p,* long *o,* long *a, h, y* (long-*i* sound), *d*

**Lesson focus word:** *Go*

## Sign Description

Curl the fingers of your left hand to form a *g* shape, as illustrated. Place your hand against your throat to feel the guttural vibrations while making the hard-*g* sound.

## Procedures

1. Demonstrate the *g* sign, making the hard-*g* sound as the sign is made.

2. Review the long-*o* sign.

3. Demonstrate blending the *g* and *o* signs to make the word *go.*

## Student Page – #17

**TEXT:** See us go.

**ILLUSTRATION:** Draw a picture of your horse running.

## Extension Activity

**WORD CHALLENGE:** *bug, dug, game, gape, grade, grain, grape, gray, greed, gripe, grub, grump, gum, Gus, hug, mug, rug*

## Enrichment Activities

*G* **SONG** (sung to the tune of "Twinkle, Twinkle, Little Star"):

Curl your thumb, and you will see
You have made the letter *g*.
Put your *g* up to your throat,
Then say words like *g-g-goat*.
You can feel that hard-*g* sound
Every time the *g* comes 'round.

**LOOKING UP:** Students lie on their backs, make the *g* sign, and repeat words pronounced by the teacher that contain the hard-*g* sound.

## Student Take-Home Book—*Gray Bug*

# LESSON 18 – *j*

**Previously taught letters:** long *e, m, s, w,* short *u,* long *i, b, n* (and silent *e*), *z, r, p,* long *o,* long *a, h, y* (long-*i* sound), *d, g*

**Lesson focus word:** *Jump*

## Sign Description

Draw the *j* shape in the air with the index finger of your left hand while making the *j* sound.

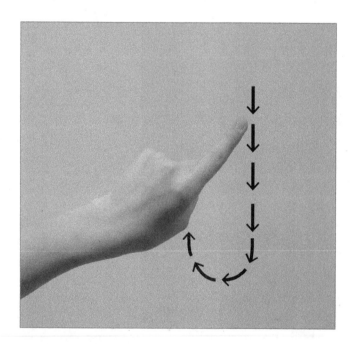

## Procedures

1. Demonstrate the *j* sign, making the *j* sound as the sign is made.

2. Review the *u, m,* and *p* signs.

3. Demonstrate blending the *j, u, m,* and *p* signs to make the word *jump*.

## Student Page – #18

**TEXT:** See us jump.

**ILLUSTRATION:** Draw a picture of your horse jumping over something.

## Extension Activities

**WORD CHALLENGE:** *jade, Jane, Jay, Jeep, Jo, Joe, jug*

**JUMPING-*J* RELAY:** Divide the class into teams for a relay. The first person on each team must jump from the team's starting point to its destination point and back. Each child must make the *j* sign and sound with each jump.

## Enrichment Activity

**JIGGLERS:** Make Jell-O jigglers for snack.

## Student Take-Home Book—*Little Girls*

# LESSON 19 – *f*

**Previously taught letters:** long *e*, *m*, *s*, *w*, short *u*, long *i*, *b*, *n* (and silent *e*), *z*, *r*, *p*, long *o*, long *a*, *h*, *y* (long-*i* sound), *d*, *g*, *j*

**Lesson focus word:** *Fun*

## Sign Description

Draw the letter *f* on your left hand with a washable marker, as illustrated. Place your hand in front of your lips while making the *f* sound.

## Procedures

1. Demonstrate the *f* sign, making the *f* sound as the sign is made.

2. Review the *u* and *n* signs.

3. Demonstrate blending the *f*, *u*, and *n* signs to make the word *fun*.

## Student Page – #19

*Note: Introduce the upper-case* F *before beginning the student page.*

**TEXT:** Fun, fun, fun.

**ILLUSTRATION:** Draw a picture of you and your friends smiling as you ride your horse.

## Extension Activities

**WORD CHALLENGE:** *fade, fame, fee, feed, fine, for, frame, fray, freed, freeze, fry, fuss, fuzz*

**SLOW RACE:** Have a **race** to see who can be the last to finish making the *f* sign (and *f* sound). Call time after 30 seconds. All students still making the *f* sound when time is called are winners.

*FE, FI, FO, FUM:* Read "Jack and the Beanstalk." Students can sign *Fe, Fi, Fo, Fum* when it is read.

## Enrichment Activity

**FAVORITE THINGS:** Play a recording of the song "My Favorite Things" (from *The Sound of Music*). Direct the class in rewriting the song to contain favorite things that begin with the letter *f.* For example:

Footballs and fossils and feathers and faces,
Foxes and Frisbees and fantastic places,
French fries and fiddles and farm bells that ring …
These are a few of my favorite things.

## Student Take-Home Book—*Fe, Fi, Fo, Fum*

# LESSON 20 – *t*

**Previously taught letters:** long *e, m, s, w,* short *u,* long *i, b, n* (and silent *e*), *z, r, p,* long *o,* long *a, h, y* (long-*i* sound), *d, g, j, f*

**Lesson focus word:** *Time*

## Sign Description

Make the horizontal portion of the *t* shape with the index finger of your left hand, as illustrated, then make the vertical portion with the right hand. Gently tap the two fingers together while making the *t* sound. Remove the right hand. Explain that in the future only the left hand (the horizontal portion of the *t*) will be used to make the sign, as the index finger of the left hand strikes an *imaginary* vertical portion of the *t*.

## Procedures

1. Demonstrate the *t* sign, making the *t* sound as the sign is made.

2. Review the long-*i* and *m* signs, as well as the silent-*e* concept.

3. Demonstrate blending the *t, i, m,* and silent-*e* signs to make the word *time.*

## Student Page – #20

**TEXT:** Time for …

**ILLUSTRATION:** Draw a picture of you and your friends sitting on the ground beside your horse.

## Extension Activities

**WORD CHALLENGE:** *beet, bite, but, date, fate, feet, gate, hate, hut, just, jut, mate, meet, note, nut, rate, rust, rut, stain, state, stay, stone, store, street, stride, tame, tape, teen, tide, tone, tore, trade, train, tray, trust, tub, tug*

**TAMBOURINE TIME:** Obtain tambourines for as many of your students as possible. Read a list of words as the children march around the room, striking the tambourine when they hear a word that begins with *t*.

**TOOTHPICK *T's*:** Students will make *t* shapes with toothpicks, then use a marker to complete a word beginning with the letter *t*.

## Enrichment Activity

**T-SHIRTS:** Students may decorate cutout T-shirt shapes with pictures of objects that begin with the letter *t*.

## Student Take-Home Book—*Gus*

# LESSON 21 – short *a*

**Previously taught letters:** long *e, m, s, w,* short *u,* long *i, b, n* (and silent *e*), *z, r, p,* long *o,* long *a, h, y* (long-*i* sound), *d, g, j, f, t*

**Lesson focus word:** *Nap*

## Sign Description

The sign for the short-*a* sound is the same as for the long *a,* except the sign should be made at eye level rather than at chest level.

## Procedures

1. Demonstrate the short-*a* sign, making the short-*a* sound as the sign is made.

2. Review the *n* and *p* signs.

3. Demonstrate blending the *n,* short-*a,* and *p* signs to make the word *nap.*

## Applicable Phonics Rule

Review Phonics Rule 3.

## Student Page – #21

**TEXT:** a nap.

**ILLUSTRATION:** Draw a picture of you and your friends sleeping.

## Extension Activities

**WORD CHALLENGE:** *am, bad, bag, ban, band, bat, brass, dad, Dan, drab, drag, fan, fast, fat, gag, gap, gas, grab, grass, had, hand, hat, jam, mad, man, map, mass, mat, Nan, pad, pan, past, pat, rag, ram, ran, rap, rat, sad, sag, Sam, sat, Stan, tap, tram, trap, wag, zap*

**LONG *A*/SHORT *A*:** Read a list of words that contain either the long-*a* or short-*a* sound. Students will respond with appropriate long- or short-*a* sign.

## Enrichment Activities

***A* WHEELS:** Students may make a word wheel of the *at* word family.

**SHORT-*A* POEM** (sung to the tune of "Three Blind Mice"):

> That fat cat,
> That fat cat.
> Sat on my hat,
> Sat on my hat.
> He sat on my hat, and he mashed it flat,
> Then chased a rat with a baseball bat.
> Have you ever heard of a cat like that?
> That fat cat!

**WHAT SAT ON WHAT?** Instruct students to complete and illustrate the sentence, "A _____ sat on a _____," using words that end with *at*.

## Student Take-Home Book—*Bad Nan*

# LESSON 22 – *k*

**Previously taught letters:** long *e, m, s, w,* short *u,* long *i, b, n* (and silent *e*), *z, r, p,* long *o,* long *a, h, y* (long-*i* sound), *d, g, j, f, t,* short *a*

**Lesson focus word:** *Wake*

## Sign Description

Draw the *k* shape on your hand with a washable marker, as illustrated. Make the hard-*k* sound while doing a cutting motion with your index finger and middle finger.

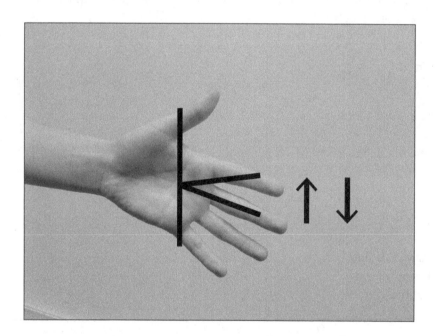

## Procedures

1. Demonstrate the *k* sign, making the *k* sound as the sign is made.

2. Review the *w* and long-*a* signs, as well as the silent-*e* concept.

3. Demonstrate blending the *w,* long-*a, k,* and silent-*e* signs to make the word *wake.*

4. Introduce the sight-word concept and the sight word *to.*

## Student Page – #22

**TEXT:** Wake up! Wake up! Time to go home.

**ILLUSTRATION:** Draw a picture of you and your friends awake.


## Extension Activities

**CUTTING *K*'s:** Cut the fingers from discarded pairs of gloves. Give two **fingers** to each child who will slip them over the index and middle fingers to resemble a pair of scissors. The students will make the *k* sign with their **scissors fingers** each time you read a word that beings with the *k* sound.

**WORD CHALLENGE:** *bake, bike, bunk, fake, fork, hike, hunk, Jake, junk, Kay, keen, keep, kite, make, Mike, musk, peek, pike, poke, rake, sake, sky, snake, spike, stake, strike, stripe, take*


## Enrichment Activity

***K* KITES:** Write on the board a list of words that begin with the letter *k*. Students may clip magazine pictures of the listed objects and glue them to a large class-sized kite.


## Student Take-Home Book—*Kay Pokes*

# LESSON 23 – *c*

**Previously taught letters:** long *e, m, s, w,* short *u,* long *i, b, n* (and silent *e*), *z, r, p,* long *o,* long *a, h, y* (long-*i* sound), *d, g, j, f, t,* short *a, k*

**Lesson focus word:** *Can*

## Sign Description

The hand position for the hard-*c* sound is similar to the *k* (see LESSON 22). Point out that the letter *c* is "hidden" inside the letter *k*. The vertical line, however, should not be drawn.

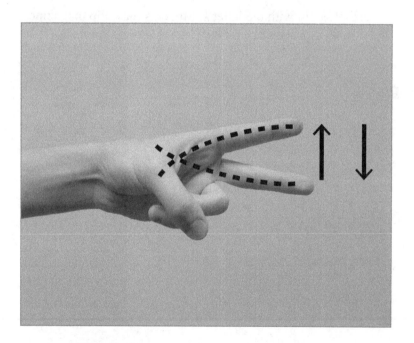

## Procedures

1. Demonstrate the hard-*c* sign, making the *k* sound as the sign is made.

2. Review the short-*a* and *n* signs.

3. Demonstrate blending the *c,* short *a,* and *n* signs to make the word *can.*

## Student Page – #23

**TEXT:** My horse can run fast.

**ILLUSTRATION:** Draw a picture of your horse running fast.

## Extension Activities

**WORD CHALLENGE:** *cab, cake, came, cane, cap, cape, care, case, cast, cat, code, cone, cope, core, crab, cram, crane, crate, creed, creep, crime, crust, cry, cub, cup*

**CK CAN TOO:** Explain that the hard-*c* sound is sometimes spelled *ck.*

**REPEAT "CUTTING *K*'s"** (see LESSON 22), calling this activity **"CUTTING *C*'s."**

## Enrichment Activity

**CRAZY CAKE:** List words on the board that begin with the hard-*c* sound. Students may list ingredients for a *crazy cake,* choosing ingredients from the list of words on the board. Students may draw a picture of their *crazy cakes.*

## Student Take-Home Book—*Can I Find?*

# LESSON 24 – *L*

**Previously taught letters:** long *e, m, s, w,* short *u,* long *i, b, n* (and silent *e*), *z, r, p,* long *o,* long *a, h, y* (long-*i* sound), *d, g, j, f, t,* short *a, k, c*

**Lesson focus word:** *Last*

## Sign Description

Glide through the shape of the upper-case letter *L* with the left hand, as illustrated, while making the *L* sound. (The upper-case *L* shape is used for the *L* sign because it is more easily recognizable than the lower-case *l*.)

## Procedures

1. Demonstrate the *L* sign, making the *L* sound as the sign is made.

2. Review the short-*a, s,* and *t* signs.

3. Demonstrate blending the *L, a, s,* and *t* signs to make the word *last*.

4. Explain that the upper- and lower-case letters are signed the same way.

## Student Page – #24

**TEXT:** Home at last.

**ILLUSTRATION:** Draw a picture of you and your friends at your house.

## Extension Activities

**WORD CHALLENGE:** *Bill, bleed, clam, clan, close, eel, flake, fleet, glad, hill, lab, lad, lame, lane, lap, late, leek, like, line, lug, pile, pill, sleep, slide, slime, stale*

**LAZY** *L:* Explain that the *L* makes a lazy sound. Students can *lazily* make the *L* sign and exaggerate the *L* sound as they repeat words beginning with *L* that you read.

## Enrichment Activity

**LUCY LOVED HER LITTLE LAMB** (sing the following song to the tune of "Mary Had a Little Lamb," making the *L* sign as each *L* is pronounced):

Lucy loved her little lamb, little lamb, little lamb;
Lucy loved her little lamb; its legs were long and low.
Everywhere that Lucy went, Lucy went, Lucy went,
Everywhere that Lucy went, the lamb was sure to go.

## Student Take-Home Book—*Lee Likes*

# LESSON 25 – short *i*

**Previously taught letters:** long *e, m, s, w,* short *u,* long *i, b, n* (and silent *e*), *z, r, p,* long *o,* long *a, h, y* (long-*i* sound), *d, g, j, f, t,* short *a, k, c, L*

**Lesson focus words:** *pig, pink, big, it, is*

## Sign Description

Make the same sign as for the long *i,* except the index finger should be held horizontally, as illustrated. Make the short-*i* sound as the sign is made.

## Procedures

1. Demonstrate the short-*i* sign, making the short-*i* sound as the sign is made.

2. Review the *p* and *g* signs.

3. Demonstrate blending the *p, i,* and *g* signs to make the word *pig.* Repeat for *big, it,* and *pink.*

## Applicable Phonics Rule

**Phonics/Spelling Rule 9:** When a word or syllable has a short vowel sound immediately followed with the sound of *k*, the *k* sound is usually spelled with the digraph *ck*. E.g., *chick, neck, stuck, tack.*

## Student Page – #25

**TEXT:** I see a pig. It is a pink pig, and it is big.

**ILLUSTRATION:** Draw a picture of a pig.

## Extension Activities

**WORD CHALLENGE:** *bid, bin, bit, bliss, brim, clip, did, dig, dim, dip, drill, fig, fill, fin, fit, fizz, flip, frill, grid, grin, grit, hid, him, hip, hit, ill, in, Jill, Jim, kick, kid, kill, Kim, kin, kiss, kit, lid, lip, mill, miss, mitt, pick, pin, pit, rib, Rick, rip, sick, sin, sip, sis, sit, slick, slid, slim, slit, stiff, still, swim, tick, Tim, tin, tip, trick, trim, trip, wig, will, win, wit*

**PICK A CARD:** One student at a time goes to the front of the room and signs a word from the list above. The student who correctly guesses the word gets to sign the next one.

**LONG *I*/SHORT *I*:** Read a list of words that contain either the long-*i* or the short-*i* sound. Students respond with the appropriate *i* sign.

**SPELL WELL:** The teacher slowly reads and signs a short word that contains the short-*i* sound. On individual chalkboards or tablets, students write the word being signed, then hold up their chalkboards/tablets so the teacher can see when they've finished writing the word.

## Enrichment Activity

**THE SHORT-*I* GAME:** On the playground one child in a group of about 10 students is designated "it." In order to avoid being tagged and becoming "it," the other students must call out a word that contains the short-*i* sound while making the short-*i* sign. Words may not be repeated.

## Student Take-Home Book—*Big Bad Pig*

# LESSON 26 – short *e*

**Previously taught letters:** long *e, m, s, w,* short *u,* long *i, b, n* (and silent *e*), *z, r, p,* long *o,* long *a, h, y* (long-*i* sound), *d, g, j, f, t,* short *a, k, c, L,* short *i*

**Lesson focus words:** *pet, let, wet*

## Sign Description

The sign for short *e* is made like the long-*e* sign, except the hand is held at eye level rather than at chest level. Make the short-*e* sound as the sign is made.

## Procedures

1. Demonstrate the short-*e* sign, making the short-*e* sound as the sign is made.

2. Review the *p, t, w,* and *L* signs.

3. Demonstrate blending the signs to make the words *pet, let,* and *wet.*

## Student Page – #26

**TEXT:** It is my pet pig. I let my pet play in wet mud.

**ILLUSTRATION:** Draw a picture of your pet pig playing in the mud.

## Extension Activities

**WORD CHALLENGE:** *bed, beg, bell, Ben, Bess, best, bet, bled, bless, deck, den, dress, fed, fell, fled, Fred, fret, hem, hen, Jed, jell, jest, jet, keg, led, leg, less, let, Meg, men, mess, met, neck, Ned, Nell, nest, net, peck, pen, pep, pled, press, rest, sell, set, sled, stem, step, swell, Ted, tell, ten, test, web, zest*

**LONG *E*/SHORT *E*:** Read a list of words that contain either the long-*e* or the short-*e* sound. Students respond by making the appropriate *e* sign.

**MAKE-A-WORD:** Write the following letters on individual index cards and distribute two cards to each student in the following combinations: *b & d; b & g; b & ll; b & t; d & ll; f & d; f & ll; g & t; L & g; L & t; m & g; m & t; n & t; p & g; p & n; p & p; p & t; r & d; s & ll, s & t; t & d; t & ll; t & n; v & t; w & d; w & t;* and *w & ll*. Place an index card on which the letter *e* has been written in the chalk tray. One child at a time takes his/her cards to the board and places one card before the *e* and the other card after the *e* to make a word. The other students sign and read the completed word.

## Enrichment Activity

**SHORT-*E* PUZZLES:** Put the cards used in the MAKE-A-WORD activity into individual Ziploc bags and place them in an activity center. Allow each student in the center to make word puzzles by using the index cards to create words around a large letter *e* drawn in the center of a sheet of paper.

## Student Take-Home Book—*A Big Egg*

# LESSON 27 – *sh*

**Previously taught letters:** long *e, m, s, w,* short *u,* long *i, b, n* (and silent *e*), *z, r, p,* long *o,* long *a, h, y* (long-*i* sound), *d, g, j, f, t,* short *a, k, c, L,* short *i,* short *e*

**Lesson focus word:** *She*

## Sign Description

Hold your extended index finger vertically in front of your lips, as illustrated, while making the *sh* sound.

## Procedures

1. Demonstrate the *sh* sign, making the *sh* sound as the sign is made.

2. Review the long-*e* sign.

3. Demonstrate blending the *sh* and *e* signs to make the word *she.*

## Phonics Reminder

Review digraphs and color code *sh* red. Remind students that red means to *stop and think*.

## Student Page – #27

**TEXT:** She is a mess.

**ILLUSTRATION:** Draw a picture of your pet pig covered with mud.

## Extension Activities

**WORD CHALLENGE:** *brush, cash, crash, dash, dish, fish, flash, gash, sash, shack, shade, shame, shape, sheep, sheet, shelf, shell, shine, ship, shock, shore, short, trash*

**S OR SH?** As you read the following list of words, the students will make the sign of the beginning sound, either *s* or *sh*: *sell, see, she, same, sack, sad, shake, sake, sham, Sam, sheen, seen, seep, shelf, self, shift, sift, shin, sin, sip, sock, sort, shag,* and *sag*.

## Enrichment Activities

**HEAD AND SHOULDERS, SHOES AND SHINS** (sing to the tune of "Head and Shoulders, Knees and Toes," pointing to the appropriate body part as each part is named):

Head and shoulders, shoes and shins, shoes and shins,
Head and shoulders, shoes and shins, shoes and shins;
Our shirts and shorts and shampoo too (point to hair) …
Head and shoulders, shoes and shins, shoes and shins.

**SH-SH-SH-SH:** Explain that the *sh* sound usually indicates a request for others to be very quiet. Instruct the students to sit quietly in a circle on the carpet and softly make the *sh* sound. One student at a time names a word that begins with *sh* until all students have responded.

## Student Take-Home Book—*A Fish for a Sheep*

# LESSON 28 – *er/ir/ur*

**Previously taught letters:** long *e*, *m*, *s*, *w*, short *u*, long *i*, *b*, *n* (and silent *e*), *z*, *r*, *p*, long *o*, long *a*, *h*, *y* (long-*i* sound), *d*, *g*, *j*, *f*, *t*, short *a*, *k*, *c*, *L*, short *i*, short *e*, *sh*

**Lesson focus word:** *Girl*

## Sign Description

Rotate the index finger of your left hand in the air, as illustrated, while making the *er/ir/ur* sound. Move your finger in an upward spiral. Explain that the index finger is tw*ir*ling in the air.

## Procedures

1. Demonstrate the *er/ir/ur* sign, making the *er/ir/ur* sound as the sign is made.

2. Review the *g* and *L* signs.

3. Demonstrate blending the *g*, *er/ir/ur*, and *L* signs to make the word *girl*.

4. Introduce the sight word *one*.

5. Optional modification: Demonstrate *ir* by twirling the *i* sign in the air while making the *er/ir/ur* sound. Demonstrate *er* by twirling the *e* sign in the air while making the *er/ir/ur* sound. Demonstrate *ur* by twirling the *u* sign in the air while making the *er/ir/ur* sound. (This promotes correct spelling of *er, ir,* and *ur* words.)

## Student Page – #28

**TEXT:** My pig is a girl. Her name is Furl. One day Furl ran away.

**ILLUSTRATION:** Draw a picture of your pet pig running away.

## Extension Activities

**WORD CHALLENGE:** *Bert, bird, blurt, burn, burst, curb, curd, curt, dirt, fern, fir, firm, first, flirt, her, herd, hurl, hurt, jerk, lurk, nurse, perk, purr, purse, shirt, sir, stern, term, terse, turn, twirl*

**WORD DETECTIVES:** Tell the students that detectives look for clues to help them figure things out. Explain that they will be word detectives and look for such clues as *er, ir,* or *ur* to help them read words. Write a WORD CHALLENGE word on the board. Allow a student to circle with colored chalk the *e/i/u-r* combinations. The remainder of the students should make the *e/i/u-r* sign if the circle is drawn correctly. Slowly sign and read the word with the class. Repeat with additional WORD CHALLENGE words. (Exceptions such as *word* and *world* should be taught later as sight words.)

## Enrichment Activity

**BIRDS OF A FEATHER:** Prepare a board containing pockets labeled *er, ir,* and *ur.* Pockets can be decorated to look like feathers. Print each of the words used in the WORD CHALLENGE, then place them in the appropriate pocket. Label the board "Birds of a Feather."

## Student Take-Home Book—*Burt Flirts*

# LESSON 29 – short *o*

**Previously taught letters:** long *e, m, s, w,* short *u,* long *i, b, n* (and silent *e*), *z, r, p,* long *o,* long *a, h, y* (long-*i* sound), *d, g, j, f, t,* short *a, k, c, L,* short *i,* short *e, sh, er/ir/ur*

**Lesson focus words:** *got, hot*

## Sign Description

Hold your left hand at eye level, make an *o* shape, as illustrated, then make the short-*o* sound.

## Procedures

1. Demonstrate the short-*o* sign, making the short-*o* sound as the sign is made.

2. Review the *g, h,* and *t* signs.

3. Demonstrate blending the signs to make the words *got* and *hot.*

4. Introduce the sight word *was.*

## Student Page – #29

**TEXT:** It was a summer day. My pig got hot. She went to sleep.

**ILLUSTRATION:** Draw a picture of your pet pig asleep.

## Extension Activities

**WORD CHALLENGE:** *blob, block, blot, bog, bop, clock, clod, clog, clop, clot, cob, cod, cog, cop, cot, crock, crop, dock, dog, doll, Don, dot, drop, frog, gob, God, hog, hop, job, jog, Josh, jot, lock, log, lot, mob, mock, mom, mop, not, odd, off, plod, plop, plot, pod, pop, pot, prod, prom, prop, rob, rock, rod, rot, shock, shod, shop, shot, slop, slosh, slot, sob, sock, sod, sop, stock, stop, Tom, top, tot*

**WHAT DO YOU SEE?** Write the following words on the board, signing and reading each word with the class. Allow students to make generalizations as to why certain words contain the short-*o* sound, while others contain long *o: cop, cope, dot, dote, hop, hope, mop, mope, not, note, rob, robe, rod, rode, tot,* and *tote.*

## Enrichment Activity

**MAGNETIC WORDS:** Prepare two sets of magnetic letters, each set containing all of the previously taught consonants and the letter *o.* Place each set on a magnetic surface for the whole class to see. Read and sign a word containing the short *o,* allowing one student from each of two teams to race to rearrange the letters and spell the word. Repeat with additional words from the WORD CHALLENGE list.

## Student Take-Home Book—*Mom Shops*

# LESSON 30 – *th*

**Previously taught letters:** long *e, m, s, w,* short *u,* long *i, b, n* (and silent *e*), *z, r, p,* long *o,* long *a, h, y* (long-*i* sound), *d, g, j, f, t,* short *a, k, c, L,* short *i,* short *e, sh, er/ir/ur,* short *o*

**Lesson focus words:** *thin, thick, with*

## Sign Description

Pretend to touch the tip of your tongue with your index finger while making the *th* sound.

## Procedures

1. Demonstrate the *th* sign, making the *th* sound as the sign is made.

2. Review the short-*i, n, ck,* and *w* signs.

3. Demonstrate blending the signs to make the words *thin, thick,* and *with.*

## Phonics Reminder

Color code the digraph *th* red.

## Student Page – #30

**TEXT:** A thin sheep with thick hair came by. The thin sheep sat by the pig.

**ILLUSTRATION:** Draw a picture of a thin sheep looking at the sleeping pig.

## Extension Activity

**WORD CHALLENGE:** *Beth, both, path, than* (briefly point out the fact that *th* makes two sounds), *thank, that, then, think, third, thirst, this, thorn, those* (approximate the *s* sound), *thud, thump, thus, thy, with*

## Enrichment Activity

**YUMMY *TH*:** Instruct all students to wash their hands thoroughly. Give each child a small quantity of pudding. At your signal all students dip the tips of the index fingers of their left hands into the pudding. When someone thinks of a word that contains the *th* sound, he/she calls it out, then everyone says the word and touches his/her tongue while making the *th* sound. (Stress the fact that normally we do not actually touch our tongues to make this sign.)

## *Student Take-Home Book—The Dog's Birthday*

# LESSON 31 – *ing*

**Previously taught letters:** long *e, m, s, w,* short *u,* long *i, b, n* (and silent *e*), *z, r, p,* long *o,* long *a, h, y* (long-*i* sound), *d, g, j, f, t,* short *a, k, c, L,* short *i,* short *e, sh, er/ir/ur,* short *o, th*

**Lesson focus words:** *going, sleeping*

## Sign Description

Review the signs for short-*i, n,* and *g.* Demonstrate blending the three signs into one fluid motion; only hint at the *n* sign as your hand moves from the short-*i* to the *g* position. The *ing* sign becomes a single, rapid movement.

## Procedures

1. Demonstrate the *ing* sign, making the *ing* sound as the sign is made.

2. Review the *g,* long-*o, s, L, e,* and *p* signs.

3. Demonstrate blending the signs to make the words *going* and *sleeping.*

## Phonics Reminder

Color code the *ing* chunk for visual emphasis.

## Student Page – #31

**TEXT:** But the pig kept sleeping, so the sheep got up and kept going.

**ILLUSTRATION:** Draw a picture of the sheep walking away.

## Extension Activities

**WORD CHALLENGE:** *bagging, batting, betting, blasting, bleeding, blessing, blinding, blurting, brimming, bring, bringing, bumping, burning, capping, casting, clapping, cling, clipping, clothing, creeping, crying, curling, dashing, digging, dimming, ding, dinging, dipping, dragging, dressing, drilling, dropping, drumming, drying, fasting, feeding, filling, finding, fishing, flapping, fling, flinging, flirting, flunking, freeing, fretting, frying, fussing, going, grabbing, grinning, grubbing, grumping, hitting, hemming, hopping, hugging, humming, hurting, jerking, jogging, jumping, jutting, keeping, kicking, kidding, killing, king, kissing, lacking, lapping, laying, letting, logging, lumping, mapping, mashing, missing, mopping, napping, packing, passing, patting, paying, pecking, peeking, peeling, peeping, petting, ping, pinging, planning, playing, popping, praying, pressing, prying, pumping, ramming, resting, ring, ringing, robbing, rotting, rubbing, running, rusting, sagging, saying, seeing, seeding, seeking, seeping, selling, setting, shipping, shocking, shopping, singing, sipping, sitting, slamming, slapping, sledding, sleeting, slimming, sling, slinging, slumping, sobbing, stabbing, staying, stemming, stepping, stocking, stopping, swelling, swimming, swing, swinging, tagging, tanning, tapping, telling, testing, thing, thinking, tipping, tracking, trapping, trimming, trucking, trusting, trying, tugging, turning, twirling, wagging, weeding, weeping, willing, wing, winging, winning, wishing, zing, zinging*

**ADDING ON:** Call out a verb such as *run*. The class repeats the word, adding and signing *ing*.

**THE MATCHING GAME:** Give large cards on which *ing* is written to half of your students. The other students are given cards on which one of the following consonants or blends is written: *br, d, fl, k, p, r, s, sl, spr, sw, th, w,* or *z*. Review the sign of each letter as the cards are distributed. Each child will attempt to find a partner whose "word part" will combine with his/hers to create a word.

## Enrichment Activity

The sign for *ing* is a combination of the signs for *i, n,* and *g.* Allow advanced students to create their own shortcut sign for other common letter combinations such as *i, n,* and *k.*

## Student Take-Home Book—*A Wedding Day*

# LESSON 32 – *x*

**Previously taught letters:** long *e*, *m*, *s*, *w*, short *u*, long *i*, *b*, *n* (and silent *e*), *z*, *r*, *p*, long *o*, long *a*, *h*, *y* (long-*i* sound), *d*, *g*, *j*, *f*, *t*, short *a*, *k*, *c*, *L*, short *i*, short *e*, *sh*, *er/ir/ur*, short *o*, *th*, *ing*

**Lesson focus words:** *fox*, *next*

## Sign Description

Cross the index and middle finger of your left hand to roughly form an *x* shape, as illustrated.

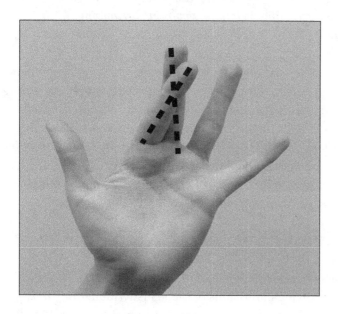

## Procedures

1. Demonstrate the *x* sign while making the *x* sound.

2. Review the *f*, short-*o*, *n*, short-*e*, and *t* signs.

3. Demonstrate blending the signs to make the words *fox* and *next*.

4. Introduce the sight words *you* and *said*.

## Student Page – #32

**TEXT:** Next a fox came by. "You need a bath," she said. The fox kept running, and the pig kept sleeping.

**ILLUSTRATION:** Draw a picture of a fox talking to the pig.

## Extension Activities

**WORD CHALLENGE:** *ax, box, fix, mix, ox, sax, six*

**X RACE:** Prepare flashcards for, and review, the words *box, fix, fox, next,* and *ox.* Call one student to the front of the class. When you flash one of the *x*-word cards, the class attempts to read the word before the student at the front can cross his/her fingers to make the *x* sign.

**FIX IT:** Call three students to the front of the room. Assign each of the three students one letter from the word *six* and line them up so the word is spelled from left to right facing the class. Instruct each of the three students, beginning with the one holding the letter *s,* to sign his/her letter and make the letter sound. The rest of the class guesses the word. Repeat with other WORD CHALLENGE words.

## Enrichment Activity

**FANCY EXIT:** Instruct students to paint decorative EXIT signs, which will be displayed around the inside of the classroom exit door.

## Student Take-Home Book—*Fox Tricks*

# LESSON 33 – long *u*

**Previously taught letters:** long *e, m, s, w,* short *u,* long *i, b, n* (and silent *e*), *z, r, p,* long *o,* long *a, h, y* (long-*i* sound), *d, g, j, f, t,* short *a, k, c, L,* short *i,* short *e, sh, er/ir/ur,* short *o, th, ing, x*

**Lesson focus words:** *cute, mule*

## Sign Description

Make the short-*u* sign (see LESSON 5). Then extend your hand and forearm forward as if pointing to someone while making the long-*u* sound. Associate the sign with the sound of the word *you.* (Explain that it normally is not polite to point, but this is an exception.)

## Procedures

1. Demonstrate the long-*u* sign, making the long-*u* sound as the sign is made.

2. Review the *m, L, c,* silent-*e,* and *t* signs.

3. Demonstrate blending the signs to make the words *cute* and *mule.*

4. Discuss the -*ed* suffix. Explain that this suffix is signed as a chunk (short *e* and *d*). (It can be explained at a later date that the -*ed* suffix sometimes makes either the *d* or *t* sound.)

## Student Page – #33

**TEXT:** A cute mule trotted up to the pig. "Hi, pig. You are cute, but you need a bath," he said. Then the mule kept going, and the pig kept sleeping.

**ILLUSTRATION:** Draw a picture of a mule talking to the pig.

## Extension Activities

**WORD CHALLENGE:** *cute, flute, June, muse, mute, tune, use*

**THINGS WE USE:** Discuss the sign for the word *use* (signed long *u, s,* silent *e;* the *s* sound should be approximated). Label a display "Things We Use." Instruct the students to clip a magazine picture of an item they sometimes use. One at a time the children go to the front of the room and sign "I use _____," signing the word *use* and filling in the blank with the name of the item in the picture.

## Enrichment Activity

**UNITE:** Discuss and sign the word *unite,* stressing the *u* sound at the beginning. Instruct students to wander around in a cleared space in the room as music is played softly. When you say the word *unite,* they are to make the *u* sign and sound, ending it with a left-handed handshake with someone nearby. Anyone without a partner after 15 seconds is out of the game.

## Student Take-Home Book—*The Mule*

# LESSON 34 – *y* (long *e*)

**Previously taught letters:** long *e, m, s, w,* short *u,* long *i, b, n* (and silent *e*), *z, r, p,* long *o,* long *a, h, y* (long-*i* sound), *d, g, j, f, t,* short *a, k, c, L,* short *i,* short *e, sh, er/ir/ur,* short *o, th, ing, x,* long *u*

**Lesson focus words:** *pony, Tony, funny*

## Sign Description

Make a *y* shape with the left hand at chest level. Quickly close the fingers to convert the *y* shape into an *e* shape as the long-*e* sound is made. Explain that *y* sometimes sounds like long *e* when it comes at the end of a word.

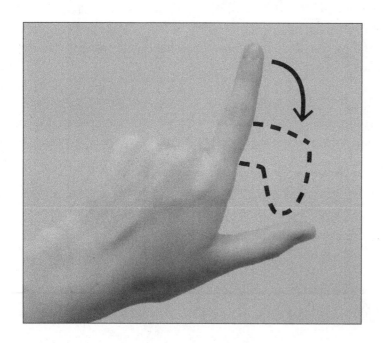

## Procedures

1. Demonstrate the *y* (long-*e*) sign, making the *y* (long-*e*) sound as the sign is made.

2. Review the *p,* long-*o, n, t, f,* and short-*u* signs.

3. Demonstrate blending the signs to make the words *pony, Tony,* and *funny.*

78

## Applicable Phonics Rule

**Phonics Rule 10:** When *y* comes at the end of a word that has another vowel, *y* says long *e*. E.g., *happy, pretty.*

## Student Page – #34

**TEXT:** A pony named Tony trotted up. "That pig smells funny," he said. Then the pony kept going, and the pig kept sleeping.

**ILLUSTRATION:** Draw a picture of a pony named Tony talking to the pig.

## Extension Activity

**WORD CHALLENGE:** *batty, buddy, buggy, bumpy, bunny, clammy, crabby, creepy, crusty, curly, daddy, Danny, dirty, dolly, fatty, fishy, flabby, flirty, floppy, frilly, funny, fussy, fuzzy, grassy, greedy, gritty, grubby, grumpy, gummy, hilly, jerky, jumpy, junky, lucky, lumpy, messy, misty, mommy, muddy, perky, puppy, runny, rusty, silly, sleepy, sticky, sunny, tacky, thorny, tricky*

## Enrichment Activity

**ADD-A-*Y*:** Read a list of words to which the letter *y* can be added at the end (base words from the WORD CHALLENGE list). Students repeat the words, adding the *e* sound while making the *y* sign. For example, when you say *fun*, the students will say *funny* while making the *y* (long-*e*) sign.

## Student Take-Home Book—*Dolly and Molly*

# LESSON 35 – *ow/ou*

**Previously taught letters:** long *e, m, s, w,* short *u,* long *i, b, n* (and silent *e*), *z, r, p,* long *o,* long *a, h, y* (long-*i* sound), *d, g, j, f, t,* short *a, k, c, L,* short *i,* short *e, sh, er/ir/ur,* short *o, th, ing, x,* long *u, y* (long-*e* sound)

**Lesson focus words:** *cow, frown, wow, brown, now*

## Sign Description

Shake your hand, as if in pain, while making the *ow/ou* sound.

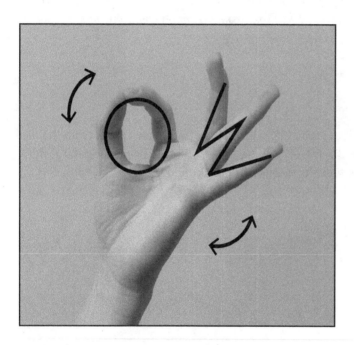

## Procedures

1. Demonstrate the *ow/ou* sign, making the *ow/ou* sound as the sign is made.

2. Review the signs for hard *c, fr, n, w,* and *br.*

3. Demonstrate blending the signs to make the words *cow, frown, wow, brown,* and *now.*

**TEXT:** A cow came by and said with a frown, "Wow. How did a pink pig get so brown? You need a bath now."

Then the cow kept going, and the pig kept sleeping.

**ILLUSTRATION:** Draw a picture of a cow talking to the pig.

## Extension Activities

**WORD CHALLENGE:** *bound, brow, cloud, crowd, crown, down, drown, flour, flower, found, gown, growl, hound, how, howl, jowl, loud, louse, mound, mouse, mouth, noun, our, out, owl, pound, pout, plow, pow, power, proud, prowl, round, rout, shout, shower, sound, south, stout, tower, town, trout, wound*

**HOW NOW, BROWN COW:** List the words *now*, *how*, and *cow* on the board, then practice their signs with the class. Tell the students that they are to sign the words as you read them in random order. Explain that your pace will get faster and faster as you read—and they should try to keep up with you. After several tries, additional words (such as *wow* and *pow*) can be added to the list.

## Enrichment Activity

**A TROUT THAT SHOUTS AND POUTS:** Write the following poem on a chart and read it with the class. On the second reading instruct the students to make the *ow/ou* sign when a word containing that sound is read:

What is your book about? My book is about a trout …
A trout that shouts and pouts: That's what my book is about.

## Student Take-Home Book—*In a Tree*

# LESSON 36 – *wh*

**Previously taught letters:** long *e, m, s, w,* short *u,* long *i, b, n* (and silent *e*), *z, r, p,* long *o,* long *a, h, y* (long-*i* sound), *d, g, j, f, t,* short *a, k, c, L,* short *i,* short *e, sh, er/ir/ur,* short *o, th, ing, x,* long *u, y* (long-*e* sound), *ow/ou*

**Lesson focus words:** *white, whiskers, whisper, why, when*

## Sign Description

Make a *w* shape with the three middle fingers of your left hand. Fan the *w* shape across your face as you make the *wh* sound, so that the force of air can be felt on your fingers as they cross in front of your lips.

## Procedures

1. Demonstrate the *wh* sign, making the *wh* sound as the sign is made.

2. Review the long-*i, sk, s, p, d, y* (long-*i* sound), short-*e, n,* short-*i, er,* and *t* signs, as well as the silent-*e* concept.

3. Demonstrate blending the signs to make the words *white, whiskers, whisper, why,* and *when.*

## Phonics Reminder

Color code the digraph *wh* red.

## Student Page – #36

**TEXT:** A white rabbit with whiskers came hopping by. "That is a messy pig," he said. "Why are you so dirty, and when did you play in the mud?" But the pig kept sleeping, so the white rabbit kept hopping.

**ILLUSTRATION:** Draw a picture of a white rabbit talking to the pig.

## Extension Activities

**WORD CHALLENGE:** *whack, whale, wham, whap, wheel, whiff, while, whim, whine, whip, whir, whirl, whiz, whopper*

**WHISPER:** Students sit in a circle and in unison make the *wh* sign as they whisper the word *whisper.* The first student whispers his/her favorite *wh* word. Once again all students say *whisper* and make the *wh* sign. Then the second child whispers his/her favorite *wh* word, continuing until everyone has had a turn.

## Enrichment Activity

**WH RIDDLES:** Ask *wh* riddles for students to answer, giving such clues as "This *wh* word rhymes with girl," etc. Students are expected to make the *wh* sign when guessing.

## Student Take-Home Book—*Why Tom Whines*

# LESSON 37 – *y* (consonant)

**Previously taught letters:** long *e, m, s, w,* short *u,* long *i, b, n* (and silent *e*), *z, r, p,* long *o,* long *a, h, y* (long-*i* sound), *d, g, j, f, t,* short *a, k, c, L,* short *i,* short *e, sh, er/ir/ur,* short *o, th, ing, x,* long *u, y* (long-*e* sound), *ow/ou, wh*

**Lesson focus words:** *yes, yuck*

## Sign Description

Draw an imaginary *y* shape on your thumb, index finger, and palm. Point with your index finger into your mouth while making the consonant-*y* sound.

## Procedures

1. Demonstrate the consonant-*y* sign, making the consonant-*y* sound as the sign is made.

2. Review the short-*u*, *ck,* short-*e*, and *s* signs.

3. Demonstrate blending the signs to make the words *yes* and *yuck.*

## Applicable Phonics Rule

**Phonics Rule 11:** When *y* comes at the beginning of a word, it is a consonant.

## Student Page – #37

**TEXT:** A duck and her duckling came by. "Yuck," said the duck. Her duckling said, "Yes, that is a yucky pig." Then the ducks kept going, and the pig kept sleeping.

**ILLUSTRATION:** Draw a picture of a duck and her duckling talking to the pig.

## Extension Activities

**WORD CHALLENGE:** *yak, yam, yap, yell, yelling, yelp, yesterday, yet, yip, yippee, yoke, yucky, yum, yummy*

**YES OR NO?** Practice signing and reading the word *yes*. Ask a series of *yes/no* questions to which the children are expected to respond by signing *yes* or *no*.

## Enrichment Activity

**YUMMY OR YUCKY?** Each child will label half a sheet of paper *Yummy* and the other half *Yucky,* then glue pictures of foods on the side that best describes their fondness (or lack of it) for the food pictured.

## Student Take-Home Book—*Yummy or Yucky?*

# LESSON 38 – *ch*

**Previously taught letters:** long *e, m, s, w,* short *u,* long *i, b, n* (and silent *e*), *z, r, p,* long *o,* long *a, h, y* (long-*i* sound), *d, g, j, f, t,* short *a, k, c, L,* short *i,* short *e, sh, er/ir/ur,* short *o, th, ing, x,* long *u, y* (long-*e* sound), *ow/ou, wh, y* (consonant)

**Lesson focus words:** *chirp, such, chum*

## Sign Description

Make a *c* shape and move your hand to resemble a train chugging along while making the *ch* sound.

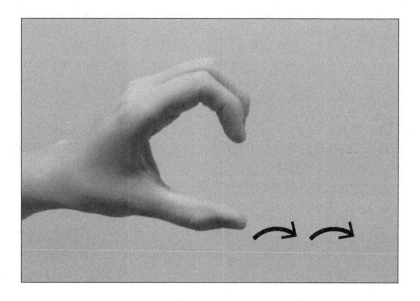

## Procedures

1.  Demonstrate the *ch* sign while making the *ch* sound.

2.  Review the *ir, p, s,* short-*u,* and *m* signs.

3.  Blend the signs to make the words *chirp, such,* and *chum.*

# Applicable Phonics Rules

**Phonics/Spelling Rule 12:** Words with a short vowel sound followed by a *ch* sound are always spelled with the trigraph *tch*. E.g., *batch, pitch*. Exceptions: *much, rich, such, which*.

**Phonics Rule 13:** Pronunciation of suffix *-ed*

a) When the root word ends with the sound of *t* or *d*, the suffix *-ed* is pronounced *ed* as in *fed*. E.g., *painted, weeded*.
b) When the root word ends with an unvoiced sound, *-ed* gives the sound of *t*. E.g., *smashed, walked, watched*.
c) When the root word ends with a voiced sound, *-ed* gives the sound of *d*. E.g., *groomed, plowed*.

*Note: Because the suffix* -ed *has three different sounds, it should be signed with the* e *and* d *signs while saying the correct sound.*

# Student Page – #38

**TEXT:** A bird hopped by. "Chirp, chirp. Such a messy chum," the bird sang. But the pig kept sleeping, so the bird kept hopping.

**ILLUSTRATION:** Draw a picture of a bird talking to the pig.

# Extension Activities

**WORD CHALLENGE:** *batch, beach, birch, breech, bunch, Chad, chap, chat, cheap, cheat, check, cheep, cheer, cheese, chill, chime, chin, chip, choke, chop, chopper, chore, chow, chubby, chum, chunk, chunky, church, ditch, kitchen, latch, leach, match, much, patch, pitch, pouch, rich, scratch, snatch*

**CH-CH TRAIN:** Label a display "Ch-Ch Train." Clip *ch* words from the newspaper. Glue words that begin with *ch* onto the engine, words with *ch* in the middle onto the center car, and words that end with *ch* onto the caboose.

**TRAIN WHISTLE:** When a student correctly names a word that begins with *ch*, blow a train whistle!

# Enrichment Activity

**SANDWICH WORDS:** Explain that *church* is a sandwich word: It begins and ends with the same letter(s). Write *ch* on a sheet of paper trimmed to resemble a slice of bread, then repeat to form the second slice of bread for a sandwich. Write the letters *ur* on paper cut to resemble bologna or another sandwich filler and display the three word parts on a board labeled "Sandwich Words." Brainstorm additional sandwich words (*dad, did, dread, maim, mom, shush, tot,* etc.).

# Student Take-Home Book—*Chubby Chad*

# LESSON 39 – *ar*

**Previously taught letters:** long *e, m, s, w,* short *u,* long *i, b, n* (and silent *e*), *z, r, p,* long *o,* long *a, h, y* (long-*i* sound), *d, g, j, f, t,* short *a, k, c, L,* short *i,* short *e, sh, er/ir/ur,* short *o, th, ing, x,* long *u, y* (long-*e* sound), *ow/ou, wh, y* (consonant), *ch*

**Lesson focus words:** *dark, far*

## Sign Description

Move your hand forward, as a wildcat might do with its paw, when roaring *ar.*

## Procedures

1. Demonstrate the *ar* sign, making the *ar* sound as the sign is made.

2. Review the *d, k,* and *f* signs.

3. Demonstrate blending the signs to make the words *dark* and *far.*

## Student Page – #39

**TEXT:** It got dark. The pig was still far from home.

**ILLUSTRATION:** Draw a picture of the pig at nighttime.

## Extension Activities

**WORD CHALLENGE:** *are, arm, bar, barb, bark, barn, Bart, car, card, cart, charm, chart, Clark, dart, farm, farmer, garb, hard, hark, harm, harp, jar, lard, lark, mark, shark, star, start, tar, tarp, tart, yarn*

**ARE YOU?** Practice reading and signing the word *are* (*ar*, silent *e*). Ask a series of questions to which the children would respond positively. The students will respond by making the *ar* sign and saying, "We are." Sample questions: "Are you ready for lunch? Are you looking forward to playing in the gym? Are you excited about going on the field trip?"

## Enrichment Activities

*AR* **CARS:** Write *ar* words on race cars. Try to accumulate enough cars to create a line long enough to reach a designated finish line.

*AR* **ART:** Read and sign the word *art* with the class. Instruct students to write the word *art* in a decorative fashion. Display the word designs near the art center.

*AR* **POEM/SONG** (sing to the tune of "Twinkle, Twinkle, Little Star"):

Twinkle, twinkle, little star,
How I wonder what you are;
Up above the world so far,
Like a headlight on my car;
Twinkle, twinkle, little star,
How I wonder what you are.

**DARTBOARD *AR* WORDS:** Introduce the word *dart*. Using child-safe darts, create a dartboard that lists *ar* words in each section. The child must pronounce the word in the section that his/her dart hits.

## Student Take-Home Book—*Shark at Sea*

# LESSON 40 – long *oo* (spelled *oo* and *ew*)

**Previously taught letters:** long *e, m, s, w, short u,* long *i, b, n* (and silent *e*), *z, r, p,* long *o,* long *a, h, y* (long-*i* sound), *d, g, j, f, t,* short *a, k, c, L,* short *i,* short *e, sh, er/ir/ur,* short *o, th, ing, x,* long *u, y* (long-*e* sound), *ow/ou, wh, y* (consonant), *ch, ar*

**Lesson focus words:** *goose, too, new, moon, soon*

## Sign Description

Form the *o* shape at chest level, same as for the long-*o* sound. Gently shake your hand while making the long-*oo* sound; explain that your hand is shaking because of the scary *oo* sound. Alternative sign: Hold your nose as if in response to a foul odor while saying *"oo."*

## Procedures

1. Demonstrate the long-*oo* sign, making the long-*oo* sound while making the sign.

2. Review the *t* sign.

3. Demonstrate blending the *t* and *oo* signs to make the word *too.*

4. Follow a similar procedure to introduce the words *goose, flew, new, moon,* and *soon.*

## Student Page – #40

**TEXT:** A goose flew by. "You are too dirty," said the goose. "The new moon will be out soon." Then the goose kept flying, and the pig kept sleeping.

**ILLUSTRATION:** Draw a picture of a goose talking to the pig.

## Extension Activities

**WORD CHALLENGE:** *bloom, boo, boom, boot, brood, broom, chew, cool, coon, coop, crew, dew, doom, drew, food, goofy, grew, groom, hoop, Jew, loon, loose, moo, mood, noon, noose, pooch, Pooh, pool, scoot, shoot, smooth, stew, stoop, tool, toot, troop, whoop, zoo, zoom*

**TOO MUCH, GOOFY:** Discuss the meaning of the word *too*. Read and sign the words *toot* and *goofy*. Allow a puppet named Goofy to guess numbers, such as the number of students in the class and the number of teachers, desks, coats, lunchboxes, etc., in the classroom. When Goofy's guess is *too* high, the children sign the word *too* and say, "Too much, Goofy."

## Enrichment Activities

**RACCOON MASKS:** Make masks out of black circles (similar to a pair of glasses with very thick rims) to resemble a raccoon mask. Instruct students to sign and read *oo* words while wearing the masks.

**TOOT—OR TOOT?** Point out that the word *toot* is spelled the same forward and backward. Brainstorm other palindromes.

**BABOONS:** Discuss baboons and read the word.

## Student Take-Home Book—*Moose and Goose*

# LESSON 41 – *v*

**Previously taught letters:** long *e, m, s, w,* short *u,* long *i, b, n* (and silent *e*), *z, r, p,* long *o,* long *a, h, y* (long-*i* sound), *d, g, j, f, t,* short *a, k, c, L,* short *i,* short *e, sh, er/ir/ur,* short *o, th, ing, x,* long *u, y* (long-*e* sound), *ow/ou, wh, y* (consonant), *ch, ar,* long *oo* (spelled *oo* and *ew*)

**Lesson focus words:** *five, dive*

## Sign Description

Make a *v* shape with the index and middle fingers of your left hand, as illustrated. Place the *v* shape on your chest, as if forming the neckline of a vest.

## Procedures

1. Demonstrate the *v* sign while making the *v* sound.

2. Review the *f, d,* silent-*e,* and long-*i* signs.

3. Blend the signs to make the words *five* and *dive*.

## Student Page – #41

**TEXT:** Five deer ran by. "You are so dirty," one deer said. "You should dive into the lake." The five deer kept running, while the pig kept sleeping.

**ILLUSTRATION:** Draw a picture of the five deer talking to the pig.

## Extension Activities

**WORD CHALLENGE:** *carve, crave, drive, grove, rave, rove, shave, starve, stove, stoves, swerve, vane, vast, veal, vest, vet, Vicky, vile, vim, vine, vote, votes, wives*

**VICTORY:** Explain how the *v* sign has been used for many years as a symbol of victory. Write a word on the board for a child to sign and read. If the child reads the word correctly, the rest of the students make a *v* sign and say, "Victory!"

## Enrichment Activities

***V* VESTS:** Make each child a vest from a brown paper grocery bag by cutting up the front, then cutting holes for the head and each arm. Each child may cover the vest with words that begin with the letter *v* or with pictures of objects, the names of which begin with *v*.

***V* VALENTINES:** Demonstrate how the letter *v* can be connected at the top to become a heart-shaped valentine. Fill a large valentine shape with *v* words clipped from newspapers or magazines.

## Student Take-Home Book—*Can a Rooster?*

# LESSON 42 – short *oo*

**Previously taught letters:** long *e, m, s, w,* short *u,* long *i, b, n* (and silent *e*), *z, r, p,* long *o,* long *a, h, y* (long-*i* sound), *d, g, j, f, t,* short *a, k, c, L,* short *i,* short *e, sh, er/ir/ur,* short *o, th, ing, x,* long *u, y* (long-*e* sound), *ow/ou, wh, y* (consonant), *ch, ar,* long *oo* (spelled *oo* and *ew*), *v*

**Lesson focus words:** *look, took, shook, brook*

## Sign Description

Form the *o* shape at ear level. Gently shake your hand while making the short-*oo* sound.

## Procedures

1. Demonstrate the short-*oo* sign, making the short-*oo* sound as the sign is made.

2. Review the *L, t, sh, br,* and *k* signs.

3. Demonstrate blending the signs to make the words *look, took, shook,* and *brook.*

## Student Page – #42

**TEXT:** An owl took a look at the pig. She shook her wings. "Just look," she said. "Go jump into the brook." The owl did not stop. She just kept flying, and the pig kept sleeping.

**ILLUSTRATION:** Draw a picture of an owl flying over the pig.

## Extension Activities

**WORD CHALLENGE:** *book, cook, crook, good, hood, hoof, hook, nook, stood, wood, woof, wool*

*OO* **RIDDLES:** List the following letters on the board: *b, c, L, n, sh,* and *t.* Ask the students riddles that begin with one of the letters listed and end with *ook.* Sample riddle: This word describes something that has pages and words in it.

## Enrichment Activity

**HOW TO COOK A ROOK:** Discuss the words *brook, nook,* and *rook,* then read the following poem:

"Just look at this book," said the rook.
The rook shook as we took a look.
"I cooked from this book in my nook by the brook …
Till I read, 'How to cook a rook.'"

## Student Take-Home Book—*Goody, Goody, Goody*

# LESSON 43 – *aw* (spelled *aw, au, a[l],* and *a[ll]*)

**Previously taught letters:** long *e, m, s, w,* short *u,* long *i, b, n* (and silent *e*), *z, r, p,* long *o,* long *a, h, y* (long-*i* sound), *d, g, j, f, t,* short *a, k, c, L,* short *i,* short *e, sh, er/ir/ur,* short *o, th, ing, x,* long *u, y* (long-*e* sound), *ow/ou, wh, y* (consonant), *ch, ar,* long *oo* (spelled *oo* and *ew*), *v,* short *oo*

**Lesson focus words:** *all, crawling, saw, walk*

## Sign Description

Hold your left hand at shoulder level with your palm facing outward. Allow your hand to drop forward (as if in disbelief) while making the *aw* sound.

## Procedures

1. Demonstrate the *aw* sign, making the *aw* sound as the sign is made.

2. Explain that *a* followed by *L* or *ll* also spells the *aw* sound, as in the word *tall.* The word *tall* is signed with the *t, aw,* and *L* signs.

3. Explain that *au* also spells the *aw* sound.

4. Review the *s, L, cr, ing, w, p,* and *k* signs.

5. Demonstrate blending the signs to make the words *all, crawling, saw,* and *Paul.* Introduce the sight words *friend* and *have.*

96

## Student Page – #43

**TEXT:** Last of all a skunk named Paul crawled up to the pig. The pig woke up. She saw the skunk. "Hello," said the pig. The skunk was glad to have a friend. "You smell nice," said the skunk. "So do you," said the pig.

**ILLUSTRATION:** Draw a picture of a skunk talking to the pig.

## Extension Activities

**WORD CHALLENGE:** *balk, call, caw, chalk, claw, dawn, draw, drawl, drawn, fall, flaw, gall, haul, hawk, jaw, law, lawn, lawyer, mall, Paul, paw, pawn, raw, shawl, slaw, stalk, stall, talk, tall, wall, Wal-Mart*

***AWE*-SOME:** Discuss the word *awe*. Sign the word with the class. Call on students one at a time to tell something that they think is *awesome*. After each response, the class makes the *aw* sign and says, "Awesome!"

## Enrichment Activity

***I* SAW E-SAW:** Read the "I Saw E-Saw" poem with the class. (Explain that E-Saw is a name that can be spelled several different ways. It is spelled differently—Esau—in the Bible.)

I saw E-Saw drawing on a seesaw.
I saw E-Saw; he saw me.

## Student Take-Home Book—*Can I?*

# LESSON 44 – *tion*

**Previously taught letters:** long *e, m, s, w,* short *u,* long *i, b, n* (and silent *e*), *z, r, p,* long *o,* long *a, h, y* (long-*i* sound), *d, g, j, f, t,* short *a, k, c, L,* short *i,* short *e, sh, er/ir/ur,* short *o, th, ing, x,* long *u, y* (long-*e* sound), *ow/ou, wh, y* (consonant), *ch, ar,* long *oo* (spelled *oo* and *ew*), *v,* short *oo, aw* (spelled *aw, au, a[l],* and *a[ll]*)

**Lesson focus words:** *notion, motion, action, vacation, nation*

## Sign Description

Because the *tion* word chunk starts with the letter *t,* we begin as if to make the *t* sign close to the face. Then we quickly move into the *sh* sign and say "shun."

## Procedures

1. Demonstrate the *tion* sign.

2. Review the *m, n,* short-*a,* hard-*c,* long-*o, v,* and long-*a* signs.

3. Demonstrate blending the signs to form the words *notion, motion, action, vacation,* and *nation.*

4. Introduce *they* and *somewhere* as sight words.

## Applicable Syllabication Rule

**Notion:** V CV nō tion—two-syllable word with VCV pattern, divided between the first vowel (*o*) and the consonant (*t*). The vowel is long. E.g., V CV.

**Inflation:** VC CV ĭn flation—three-syllable word containing a blend (*fl*) that is considered a consonant unit. The first two syllables have the VCCV pattern, which is divided between the consonant *n* and the consonant unit (*fl*). The vowel (*i*) is short. E.g., VC CV.

**Oration:** VC V or ation—this three-syllable word begins with an *r*-controlled vowel and an *r* (*or*), which stay together. Therefore, it is divided after *r*.

## Student Page – #44

**TEXT:** When the pig takes a notion to play a game, she will motion for the skunk. These friends play action games. They may even take a vacation somewhere in the nation!

**ILLUSTRATION:** Draw a picture of the skunk and the pig playing together.

## Extension Activities

**WORD CHALLENGE:** *inflation, lotion, oration, ovation, perfection, portion, potion, quotation, vocation*

**SLOW MOTION:** Practice signing the word *motion*. Discuss slow motion. With the class, sign the *m-o* in slow motion, then quickly make the *tion* sign.

## Enrichment Activity

**GROWN-UP WORDS:** Explain to your students that learning the *tion* sign will help them be able to read grown-up words. Write the following words on the board one at a time, allowing a student to circle the *tion* in each word as the class makes the *tion* sign. Pronounce each word for the class and briefly discuss the meaning of such words as *aggravation, elevation, gravitation, location, locomotion, motivation* and *rotation*.

## Student Take-Home Book—*Men in Motion*

# APPENDIX

## Soft *g*

The soft-*g* sound can be signed by forming the shape of the *g* sign with the left hand, then drawing the *j* shape in the air (rather than holding the hand at the throat) while making the soft-*g* (*j*) sound.

## Soft *c*

A teacher at Sacred Heart School, Danville, Virginia, suggested the following sign for the soft-*c* sound: Review the hard-*c* cutting motion. Explain that scissors sometimes cut paper (make the cutting motion with the left hand). Sometimes, however, scissors tear paper. (Thrust your left hand forward as if using your *scissors* fingers to tear paper.)

## Q/qu

No sign was developed for the letter *q,* but a group of second-graders at Happy Home Primary School, Rockingham County, North Carolina, developed the following sign: Explain that the letter *q* is almost always followed by a *u.* The word *queen* starts with *qu.* To make a *qu* sign, draw a circle around your face, as if you are the queen, while making the *qu* (*kw*) sound. When your left hand reaches the top of your head, form a *u* shape and put the *u* on top of your head for a crown.

# PHONICS RULES

**Phonics Rule 1:** When a word (or syllable) has only one vowel which comes at the end of the word (or syllable), the vowel is usually long. E.g., *me, tiger.*

**Phonics Rule 2:** When two vowels come together, the first one says its name, and the second one *gets quiet.* E.g., *seem, beat.*

**Phonics Rule 3:** When a word (or syllable) has only one vowel coming between consonants, the vowel is usually short. E.g., *nut, sample.*

**Phonics Rule 4:** When a single vowel is followed by one consonant and a final *e*, the first vowel is usually long, and the final *e* is silent. E.g., *mate, take.*

**Phonics Rule 5:** When two identical (or twin) consonants follow a short vowel sound, we give only one consonant sound. E.g., *buzz.*

**Phonics Rule 6:** When *s* comes between two vowels, it usually gives the sound of *z*. E.g., *nose, rose.*

**Phonics Rule 7:** When *y* comes at the end of a word, it is a vowel. Therefore, *ay* at the end of a word has the long-*a* sound and follows Phonics Rule 2: When two vowels come together, the first one says its name, and the second one *gets quiet.*

**Phonics Rule 8:** When *y* comes at the end of a word and it is the only vowel, *y* says long *i*. E.g., *by, shy, try.*

**Phonics/Spelling Rule 9:** When a word or syllable has a short vowel sound immediately followed with the sound of *k*, the *k* sound is usually spelled with the digraph *ck*. E.g., *chick, neck, stuck, tack.*

**Phonics Rule 10:** When *y* comes at the end of a word that has another vowel, *y* says long *e*. E.g., *happy, pretty.*

**Phonics Rule 11:** When *y* comes at the beginning of a word, it is a consonant.

**Phonics/Spelling Rule 12:** Words with a short vowel sound followed by a *ch* sound are always spelled with the trigraph *tch*. E.g., *batch, pitch.* Exceptions: *much, rich, such, which.*

**Phonics Rule 13:** Pronunciation of suffix *-ed*
   a) When the root word ends with the sound of *t* or *d*, the suffix *-ed* is pronounced *ed* as in *fed*. E.g., *painted, weeded.*
   b) When the root word ends with an unvoiced sound, *-ed* gives the sound of *t*. E.g., *smashed, walked, watched.*
   c) When the root word ends with a voiced sound, *-ed* gives the sound of *d*. E.g., *groomed, plowed.*

# MY BOOK

## ILLUSTRATED BY

_____

Directions: Draw a picture of yourself and something that frightens you and makes you say "eeeee."

# eeeee

Directions: Draw a picture of yourself.

# Me

Name: _____

Directions: Draw a picture of yourself doing something exciting.

# See me.

Name: _____

Directions: Draw a picture of yourself doing something exciting while
          two of your friends are watching.

# We see.

Name: _____

Directions: Draw a picture of yourself having fun with two friends.

# See us.

Name: _____          LESSON 6: long *i*

Directions: Draw a picture of yourself looking at something behind a rock.
Your friends are waiting for you to tell them what you see.

# I see ...

Directions: Draw a picture of bees flying over your head.

# bees!

Directions: Draw a picture of nine bees.

# Nine bees ...

Directions: Draw a picture of some bees, then write the word *buzz* beside
each one.

buzz.

Directions: Draw a picture of you and your friends running away from
the bees.

# Run, run!

Directions: Draw a picture of you and your friends running up a hill.

# Run up!

Directions: Draw a picture of you and your friends at the top of the hill.
You are happy because there are no bees there.

# I see no bees.

Directions: Draw a picture of a puppy.

# I see a pup.

Directions: Draw a picture of yourself petting the pup.

# Hi, pup.

Name: _____        LESSON 15: *y* (long-*i* sound)

Directions: Draw a picture of you and your horse.

# I see my horse.

Name: _____

Directions: Draw a picture of you and your friends riding your horse.

# Ride my horse.

Name: _____

Directions: Draw a picture of your horse running.

# See us go.

Directions: Draw a picture of your horse jumping over something.

# See us jump.

Name: _____           LESSON 19: *f*

Directions: Draw a picture of you and your friends smiling as you
            ride your horse.

# Fun, fun, fun.

Name: _____

Directions: Draw a picture of you and your friends sitting on the ground
             beside your horse.

# Time for ...

Directions: Draw a picture of you and your friends sleeping.

# a nap.

Directions: Draw a picture of you and your friends awake.

# Wake up! Wake up! Time to go home.

Directions: Draw a picture of your horse running fast.

# My horse can run fast.

Name: _____

Directions: Draw a picture of you and your friends at your house.

# Home at last.

Directions: Draw a picture of a pig.

# I see a pig. It is a pink pig, and it is big.

Name: _____

Directions: Draw a picture of your pet pig playing in the mud.

# It is my pet pig. I let my pet play in wet mud.

Directions: Draw a picture of your pet pig covered with mud.

# She is a mess.

Directions: Draw a picture of your pet pig running away.

# My pig is a girl. Her name is Furl. One day Furl ran away.

Directions: Draw a picture of your pet pig asleep.

# It was a summer day. My pig got hot. She went to sleep.

Directions: Draw a picture of a thin sheep looking at the sleeping pig.

# A thin sheep with thick hair came by. The thin sheep sat by the pig.

Name: _____

Directions: Draw a picture of the sheep walking away.

# But the pig kept sleeping, so the sheep got up and kept going.

Directions: Draw a picture of a fox talking to the pig.

# Next a fox came by. "You need a  bath," she said. The fox kept running, and the pig kept sleeping.

Directions: Draw a picture of a mule talking to the pig.

A cute mule trotted up to the pig. "Hi, pig. You are cute, but you need a bath," he said. Then the mule kept going, and the pig kept sleeping.

Name: _____

Directions: Draw a picture of a pony named Tony talking to the pig.

A pony named Tony trotted up. "That pig smells funny," he said. Then the pony kept going, and the pig kept sleeping.

Directions: Draw a picture of a cow talking to the pig.

A cow came by and said with a frown, "Wow. How did a pink pig get so brown? You need a bath now." Then the cow kept going, and the pig kept sleeping.

Directions: Draw a picture of a white rabbit talking to the pig.

A white rabbit with whiskers came hopping by. "That is a messy pig," he said. "Why are you so dirty, and when did you play in the mud?" But the pig kept sleeping, so the white rabbit kept hopping.

Directions: Draw a picture of a duck and her duckling talking to the pig.

A duck and her duckling came by. "Yuck," said the duck. Her duckling said, "Yes, that is a yucky pig." Then the ducks kept going, and the pig kept sleeping.

Directions: Draw a picture of a bird talking to the pig.

A bird hopped by. "Chirp, chirp. Such a messy chum," the bird sang. But the pig kept sleeping, so the bird kept hopping.

Directions: Draw a picture of the pig at nighttime.

# It got dark. The pig was still far from home.

Name: _____

Directions: Draw a picture of a goose talking to the pig.

A goose flew by. "You are too dirty," said the goose. "The new moon will be out soon." Then the goose kept flying, and the pig kept sleeping.

Directions: Draw a picture of five deer talking to the pig.

Five deer ran by. "You are so dirty," one deer said. "You should dive into the lake." The five deer kept running, while the pig kept sleeping.

Directions: Draw a picture of an owl flying over the pig.

An owl took a look at the pig. She shook her wings. "Just look," she said. "Go jump into the brook." The owl did not stop. She just kept flying, and the pig kept sleeping.

Name: _____

Directions: Draw a picture of a skunk talking to the pig.

Last of all a skunk named Paul crawled up to the pig. The pig woke up. She saw the skunk. "Hello," said the pig. The skunk was glad to have a friend. "You smell nice," said the skunk. "So do you," said  the pig.

Directions: Draw a picture of the skunk and the pig playing together.

When the pig takes a notion to play a game, she will motion for the skunk. These friends play action games. They may even take a vacation somewhere in the nation!

# INDEX OF SIGNS

**Long *a***

**Short *a***

*ar*

*aw*

*b*

**Hard *c***

*ch*

*d*

**Long *e***

**Short *e***

*er/ir/ur*

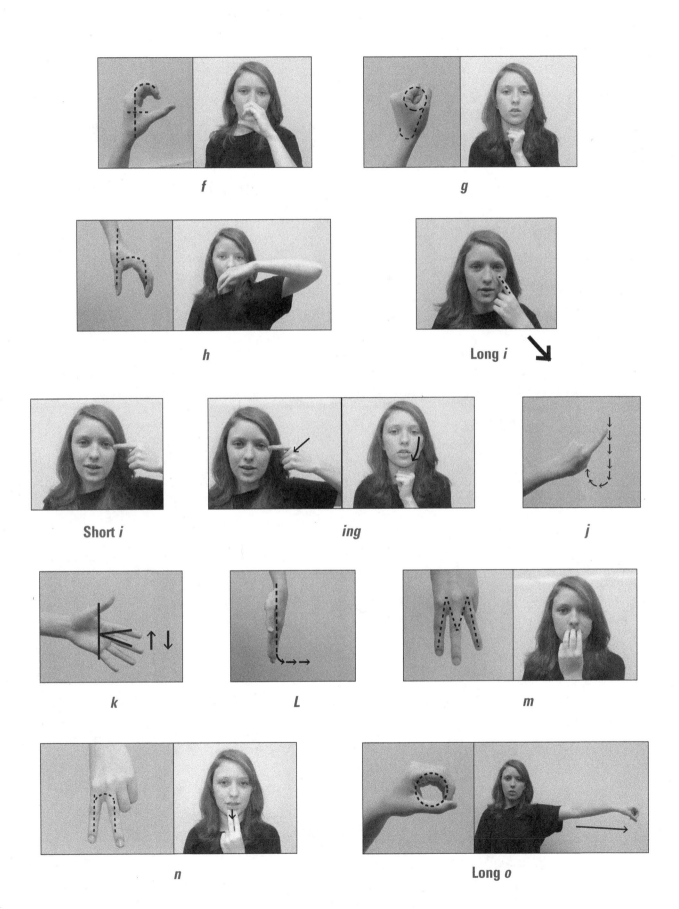

f

g

h

Long *i*

Short *i*

*ing*

*j*

*k*

*L*

*m*

*n*

Long *o*

**Short *o***

**Long *oo***

**Short *oo***

***ow/ou***

***p***

***Q/qu***

***r***

***s***

***sh***

***t***

***th***

***tion***

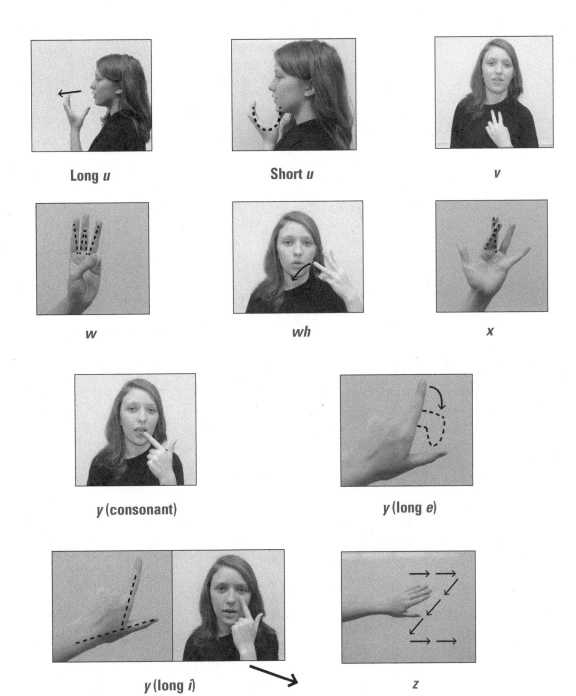

**Long u**   **Short u**   **v**

**w**   **wh**   **x**

**y (consonant)**   **y (long e)**

**y (long i)**   **z**

# WE'D LIKE TO HEAR FROM YOU!

### Join us on Facebook
www.facebook.com/rubypayne

### Respond to our blog
www.ahaprocess.com/blog

### Subscribe to our YouTube channel
www.youtube.com/ahaprocess

### Download free resources
www.ahaprocess.com

**Visit our online store for related titles by Bethanie Tucker**

- *Readiness Skills and Relationship Building for Early Childhood Education*
- *Vocabulary and Mental Model Development for Early Childhood Education*
- *Reading by Age 5*
- *Mr. Base Ten Invents Mathematics*
- *The Journey of Al and Gebra to the Land of Algebra*

**Download an eBook**

**Sign up for a one-hour SHORT COURSE online**

Meet Your Goals with Professional Development

# Solutions

For additional information, scan with your smartphone.

We have workshops, books, and other products in these areas that help you meet your needs.

| | | | | |
|---|---|---|---|---|
| **Achievement Gap (AYP)**  | **Alternative School Students**  | **Attendance/Truancy**  | **Boys: Achievement/Discipline**  | **Community Collaboration**  |
| **Decoding**  | **Discipline**  | **Dropouts/Graduation Engagement**  | **Early Childhood**  | **English Language Learners**  |
| **Gifted**  | **Higher Education**  | **Hispanic/Latino Population**  | **Interventions**  | **Leadership**  |
| **Math Elementary**  | **Math Secondary**  | **Parents**  | **Poverty/ Title I**  | **Reading/Writing**  |
| **Science**  | **Social Studies**  | **Special Education** | **Foundation Workshops** | **Online PD**  |

# Interventions

## Engage and Graduate Your Secondary Students: Preventing Dropouts

**Audience:** Recommended for teachers and administrators grades 7–12.

**Needs/issues/problems addressed:**
+ Poverty
+ Achievement gap (AYP)
+ Attendance/truancy
+ Dropouts

**Workshop Description:**
This workshop is for educators in grades 7–12 who want to design programs for student success with special emphasis on under-resourced learners.

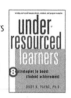

## Research-Based Strategies

**Audience:** Recommended for instructional staff (teachers, classroom paraprofessionals).

**Needs/issues/problems addressed:**
+ Poverty
+ Achievement gap (AYP)
+ Response to Intervention (RTI)

**Workshop Description:**
A teacher-friendly workshop focused on serving under-resourced students, Research-Based Strategies provides educators with hands-on techniques that help them narrow and then eliminate the achievement gap for all students, but especially under-resourced students.

## Response to Intervention (RTI)

**Audience:** Recommended for K–12 teachers and administrators.

**Needs/issues/problems addressed:**
+ Achievement gap (AYP)
+ Special education

**Workshop Description:**
Learn about the "what," the "why," and the "how" of Response to Intervention (RTI) and the under-resourced learner.

## Consulting/Academic Coaching

**Audience:** Recommended for K–12 educators.

**Needs/issues/problems addressed:**
+ Achievement gap (AYP)
+ Alternative school students
+ Poverty/Title I

**Description:**
Academic coaching is the follow-up and support provided to teachers through small group meetings. The small groups may include one or several grade levels at the elementary level, or one or several departments, or content areas at the secondary level.

**(800) 424-9484 • www.ahaprocess.com/workshops/**